A ZIONIST STAND

A
ZIONIST
STAND

Ze'ev B. Begin

FRANK CASS

First published in 1993 in Great Britain by
FRANK CASS & CO. LTD.
Gainsborough House, Gainsborough Road,
London E11 1RS, England

and in the United States of America by
FRANK CASS
c/o International Specialized Book Services, Inc.
5602 N.E. Hassalo Street
Portland, Oregon 97213

British Library Cataloguing in Publication Data

Begin, Ze'ev B.
Zionist Stand: Collected Speeches by
Ze'ev B. Begin
I. Title
956.05

ISBN 0 7146 4500 1 (hardback)
ISBN 0-7146-4089-1 (paperback)

Library of Congress Cataloging-in-Publication Data

Begin, Z.B.
    A Zionist stand : collected speeches / by Ze'ev B. Begin.
    p.   cm.
    ISBN 0-7146-4500-1 (hardback)
    ISBN 0-7146-4089-1 (paperback)
    1. Israel—Politics and government. 2. Jewish–Arab
relations—1973–   I. Title.
DS126.5.B356   1992
956.05′3—dc20   92-19891
                                                        CIP

Typeset by Regent Typesetting, London
Printed in Great Britain by BPCC Wheatons Ltd, Exeter

Contents

An Introduction to
A Zionist Stand

MY APPROACH to my fellow man rests on one foot, the same foot as that of the Gentile who learned the entire Torah from Hillel the Elder while standing on one foot: 'What is hated for yourself, do not do to your friend'. This essence is the source of man's right to equality, which is the source of his right to freedom. These are the foundations for a social programme that can be applied to all, and what was self-evident to our predecessors became obvious to a small part of humanity over the past few hundred years.

This personal stand can be expanded; the demand for equality among nations leads to the people's claim for national sovereignty over its land, in order to allow its sons to live there in freedom as do all other nations. My Zionist stand is based on the Zionist aim – the creation of a safe haven for the Jewish nation in Eretz Yisrael – and it rests on two pillars: the right of the Jewish nation to Eretz Yisrael and the right of the Jewish State to national security. From the combination of these, a policy for the State of Israel ensues, based on the prevention of foreign rule west of the Jordan River, an initiative towards establishing understanding and mutual respect between ourselves and our Arab neighbours, and efforts to reach peace treaties between the State of Israel and the Arab state.

The idea that in order to realize the Zionist aim it is necessary to apply the right of our nation to our land, is accepted today among large parts of the public both in Eretz

Yisrael and abroad. Yet, for many it is not self-understood, and for some it is even not understood. A recurring complaint is that these ideas, which were clear to Zionists two or three generations ago, 'are not rational'.

The values of man's equality and freedom are commendably upheld in free countries in peaceful times. But in moments of test, it sometimes becomes clear that citizens and their leaders have not yet totally absorbed these values, and it is difficult to use rational arguments to convince of their importance. Under the pressure of immediate events and the influence of peers advocating expedient short-range solu positive decisions sometimes resonate internal edicts and a built-in compass. These reactions are the result of a 'cultural reflex', and decisions of this kind may be considered 'irrational'. Yet, an intelligent person would not dismiss them as such, if they are rooted in the foundations of equality, freedom, truth and justice.

Such is the Zionist stand, whose foundations I have presented above. There are those who dismiss it as based on aspirations whose origin is a call of the past, not on a rational examination of difficulties in the present. I sometimes find myself envious of the children of other nations, not as ancient as our nation, not as rich with spiritual treasures, not as tied to the cradle of their heritage. Nevertheless, they have deep feelings towards their country and express a relationship that is 'self-evident'.

About a year ago I hosted a mission in the Knesset, headed by an American Congressman representing the state of Alaska, which was transferred from the Russian Czars in the 'Alaska Purchase' approximately 130 years ago. I asked him, 'How would you react if the President of the USSR were to propose, for the sake of world peace, that Alaska be leased to the USSR?' My honourable guest smiled and did not answer, as did his colleagues: it was clear that I had raised an inconceivable proposal, and that the land of Eskimos and ice, earthquakes and natural gas, whose star was added to the Stars and Stripes only about 40 years ago, that this Alaska was forever, in their eyes, an inseparable part of the United States. I reminded my guests that the 'Hebron Purchase' took place over 4,000 years ago between Abraham the Hebrew and Ephron the Hittite; that the 'Jerusalem Purchase' was concluded 3,000 years ago between David the Jew and Arava the Jebusite; I added that we have in our possession a document which testifies that in both cases our forefathers paid in cash.

My mother instilled in me a special inclination for tales of travel, stamps from faraway countries, scenic photographs, maps of the world. I have kept a notebook from my childhood, into which I copied the names of the capitals of the world and the map of Marco Polo's travels. In this notepad I found a table, drawn up in my handwriting, of the distances between cities in Eretz Yisrael. At the bottom of the table I added a footnote: 'The distance between Jerusalem and Be'er Sheva is calculated through the Hebron road, which is now occupied by the Jordanians'. I wrote these words when I was ten or twelve; Hebron had been captured by the Hashemites for five, maybe seven, years and there were those who assumed it was a 'lament for generations', but in our home this was 'self-evident'.

And not only in our home. A 'layman's atlas' was printed in those days by the 'Yavne' press. The 1949 cease-fire lines were included, but the 'West Bank' was not, and in its place was the comment, 'Trans-Jordanian-occupied land'. The author, Moshe Braver, MSc, went to great lengths to ensure that, regardless of the map's small size, long, complicated, Arabic and Hebrew names appeared: 'Jenin (Ein Ganim)', 'Tubas (Tevetz)', 'Anata (Anatot)', and in 'Egyptian-occupied land' he labelled 'Khan Unis (Chanot Yonah)'. All of that was once 'self-evident'.

3

We are in the midst of a struggle between the Jewish nation and the Arab nation over the control of Eretz Yisrael. Such a battle between two national wills will be won by him who mobilizes on a long-term basis full of the soul, and combines all tools, spiritual and material, at his command. He who appreciates pure wisdom, which convinces that 'it's time to act', as well as deep feelings which call upon him to 'get up and do'. It is perhaps to this combination that the prophet Isaiah alludes, mentioning in one verse both the spiritual ability to overcome fear and the control of the mind over courage: 'In calmness and confidence should be your bravery'.

This land is ours.

Yediot Aharonot, 28 September 1990

On Zionism and Fairness

THIS LAND is ours. 'All right, then,' my friend says, 'but isn't it true that by claiming the application of the right of the Jews to Samaria, Judaea and the Gaza district, we cause injustice to their Arab inhabitants? When we do not recognize their right to self-determination and to the establishment of an independent state – is it fair?'. 'Yes, it is fair,' I answer. 'We do not do them an injustice, because the Arab inhabitants of Samaria, Judaea and the Gaza district are not eligible for the right of self-determination.' 'What?' my startled friend compliments me, 'a person like you thinks that way, really?', and my answer is: 'Yes, really', and now let me explain my position, as a Jew from Eretz Yisrael, whose birth certificate bears the title 'Palestine – Eretz Yisrael'.

In order for a group of people to be considered a nation, to have the right to self-determination, it must be different from other groups to such an extent that would justify its separation from them. In Eretz Yisrael, on both sides of the Jordan River, within the boundaries of mandatory Palestine-Phalasteen, only two such groups live: the sons of the Arab Nation and the sons of the Jewish Nation. The Palestinian Arabs on both sides of the Jordan River are a part of the Arab Nation, even according to the first article of the 'Palestinian Charter' of the PLO. Of all nations on earth, this nation has enjoyed the fullest expression of its right to self-determination, in 20 independent Arab states with 99 per cent of the sons of the Arab Nation living in sovereign Arab states.

The Ambassador of Saudi Arabia to the United States, in an open letter to King Hussein several weeks ago, ridiculed the validity of the imperialistic boundaries of the Hashemite Kingdom of Jordan. But maybe he failed to understand that such ridicule cannot remain one-way. No reasonable person would seriously claim that the difference between the arabs of the Saud-Tribe state, called Saudi-Arabia, and the Arabs of the tribal state called the 'United Arab Emirates', is deeper than the difference between the residents of North Carolinia and the residents of South Carolina in the United States. 'But still,' says my friend, a stubborn Jew, 'maybe the Arabs of Eretz Yisrael, that is the Arabs of Palestine, are distinguished in their traits, their language and their religion, from their Arab brethren in Syria, in Iraq and in Saudi Arabia?' 'O.K., then,' I reply, myself also a stubborn Jew, 'let's assume that.'

Let us assume that. Let's assume so, although many would agree that the differences between an Italian from Milan and an Italian from Naples are deeper than the differences between an Arab in Baghdad and an Arab in Amman. But now, after we distinguish this group, for the sake of argument, from the Arab Nation, and after we refer to them in a linguistic exercise, as a 'people', the proposition is imposed upon us that out of this 'people' we should still distinguish the Arabs of Samaria–Judaea–Gaza as a separate 'people'. However, this artificial distinction must lead to the far-reaching conclusion that the Arab–Palestinian people is now separated into three different peoples: the Samarian–Judaean–Gazian Arab people in the centre, the Trans-Jordanian Arab People to the east, and the Israeli Galilean Arab people to the west. If the former has a right to self-determination, so have the other two, and in other words: one becomes three.

Something, therefore, goes wrong in the course of the transition from the generous assumptions to the severe conclusions, and the result is not merely unreasonable but it

6

is also ridiculous. An example: the Arab village of Barta'a, in the area of Nahal Iron (Wadi Arad), has been divided by the 'Green Line', which is actually the 'Line of Battle Fatigue' of the 1948–49 battles. If we accept the proposition that in the last 23 years a 'Palestinian People' has been created, precisely in the area stretching between the meandering Jordan River and the winding Green Line, then we will reach the following conclusion: the inhabitants of Barta'a-East (the 'Palestinians') belong to the new people, being different from their relatives, their own kin and folks, who live in Barta'a-West, the latter now belonging to the 'Israeli–Arab' people, or something of that sort. Confusing? Well, not only to us. Several months ago I watched the British newscast of Arab violence in the State of Israel, and I heard the amazed commentator telling his listeners: 'These stone-throwers are not Palestinians! These are Israeli Arabs!' But had he taken the time to ask one of these Arabs about his identity, he would have heard him using the following self-definition: 'I am a Palestinian Arab, a citizen of Israel'. And he would be right: the sons of one family living in Umm al Fahm (Israel), in Jenin (Samaria), and in Trans-Jordan cannot possibly belong to three different nations. That's nonsense.

'But,' insists my friend, 'they fight us, and you tell them that they are not a people? They are ready to sacrifice their lives, and isn't that sufficient proof?' 'No,' I too insist, 'that is not sufficient proof, especially in the Middle East. By that argument, the Middle East would have been shattered to pieces: a piece to the Lebanese-Christian-Arabs led by Michel Aoun; a piece to the Lebanese-Christian-Arabs led by Samir Jaja; a fragment to the Lebanese-Shiite Muslim-Arabs of "Amal", and a fragment to the Lebanese-Shiite-Muslim-Arabs of Hizb'Allah. No point is proved by the point of the dagger.'

In Eretz Yisrael, in Palestine-Phalasteen two states were

7

established: one Arab, one Jewish. There is no group of Arabs, which is different and distinguished and distinct, which is eligible, on the basis of the principle of self-determination, to establish, west of the Jordan River, an additional Arab state. 'But, still,' my friend continues to insist, 'even if it is not right, maybe it is worthwhile for us to let them have an independent Arab state in Samaria, Judaea and the Gaza district, thus getting rid of them and solving our troubles?'

Of all appropriate answers, it is possible to respond in line with the arguments of the proponents of a new partition of Western Eretz Yisrael, those who claim that the Arab violence directed towards us proves that it is impossible to prevent the establishment of an independent state from a group of people who claim that they are a nation. He who claims this should explain, then, how exactly the national aspirations of the Arabs of Eretz Yisrael, would be blocked precisely on the curves of the Green Line? How, after the realization of the 'Palestinian' national aspirations in the area of Binyamin, one would prevent their expansion from the Arabs in Ramallah to the Arabs in Jerusalem? How, immediately after the establishment of an independent Arab state west of the Jordan, can there be tranquillity betwen Jenin in Samaria and Sakhnin in the Galilee? What mechanism would then prevent some of the Galilean Arabs from trying to enforce, through the rock and the knife, through petrol bombs and television networks, the implementation of United Nations General Assembly resolution 181, recommending that the Galilee be included in an Arab State? 'Don't exaggerate,' scolds my friend. The newspaper headlines will testify that I do not.

It was 50 years ago. The most terrible of all wars started, still without actual shooting, in the Fall of 1938, when Czechoslovakia was shattered without battle by the Munich application of the right to self-determination for the Germans

8

who lived in the Sudeten hills. The British historian, A.J.P. Taylor, who died a few weeks ago, summed it up in his book *The Origins of the Second World War*:

British policy over Czechoslovakia originated in the beliefs that Germany had a moral right to the Sudeten German territory on grounds of national principle; and drew the further corollary that this victory for self determination would provide a stabler, more permanent peace in Europe ... It was a triumph for all that was best and most enlightened in British life, a triumph for those who preached equal justice between people ... With skill and persistence, Chamberlain brought first the French and then the Czechs to follow the moral line.

We must not yield today to false propaganda and 'moral' pressure, to superficiality and hypocrisy, because if we do not learn from that experience, we shall not have another opportunity. We must make an effort to reach an agreement with our Arab neighbours, based on mutual respect, an agreement which is crucial for their children and for ours. But we must not yield to the false claim that such an agreement must be based on the fictitious recognition of the 'symmetry' between the rights of the Jewish Nation and the Arab Nation in Eretz Yisrael.

With our heads held as high as our values, we should conduct this moral debate on the basis of fact and truth –

Because this land is ours.

The Jerusalem Post, 9 November 1990

Zionism and Morality – The Triple Test

SINCE THE BEGINNING of the repatriation of the Jews to Eretz Yisrael in the new era, Arabs have stood before them as an obstacle. From this confrontation ensued the moral dilemma to whose solution Ze'ev Jabotinsky has suggested a triple test, as far back as 1922. He summarized his position in a hand-written postscript in a letter written from New York, with emphasis as in the original:

The *first* question is: Do you *need* land? If you don't, if you have enough, historic rights cannot be invoked. Even if you need land, the second question would be: can the people, from whose possession you claim a portion, spare that portion; won't it leave *them* landless? This is why Japan, a 'crowded' nation, cannot in justice claim land from China which is still more 'crowded'. Only if *this* is all right, comes the third question – historic rights in support of the claim to a definite piece of territory. Such, I think, is the ethical aspect of our claim.

Seventy years later, and 41 years after the establishment of the State of Israel we can and should apply this triple test to the moral basis of our stand on the question of Eretz Yisrael, according to the reality of our times.

THE FIRST TEST: 'DO YOU *NEED* LAND?'

The Zionist aim was and still is the establishment of a safe haven for the Jewish people in Eretz Yisrael. In order to assess the connection between the national security of the State of

10

Israel and its control over Samaria and Judaea, it is fitting to quote a portion of the secret opinion submitted by the Chairman of the United States Joint Chiefs of Staff, General Earl Wheeler, to the US Secretary of Defense immediately following the Six-Day War on 29 June 1967:

Threat: The high ground running north-south through the middle of West Jordan overlooks Israel's narrow midsection and offers a route for a thrust to the sea which would split the country in two parts.

Requirements: ... as a minimum, Israel would need a defense line generally along the axis Bardala–Tubas–Nablus–Bira–Jerusalem and then to the northern part of the Dead Sea.

In other words, analysis of the threat from the east on Israel led the Joint Chiefs of Staff in 1967 to the conclusion that Israel must retain all of Judaea and most of Samaria.

In order to clarify whether this conclusion can be considered valid today, we must examine the changes that have occurred over the past 20 years in the strength of the Arab forces deployed east of the Jordan and the Arava – those of Syria, Jordan, Saudia Arabia and Iraq. These are the figures: in 1967 these countries had 1100 tanks, whereas today they have more than 11,000; in 1967 they had in their possession 400 fighter planes, whereas today they have 1600; in 1967 they had 190,000 soldiers and today there are two million soldiers armed with 7000 pieces of artillery, strengthened by 13,000 armoured personnel carriers.

It is quite clear from this comparison that those who assumed that in order to frustrate any dismembering of Israel in 1967 all of Judaea and most of Samaria must be retained, would certainly accept the conclusion that this holds true today, and all the more so. Those who claim that modern weaponry has now been developed which neutralize the value of land as a crucial element in a war, should be referred to the heads of NATO, who have reached the conclusion in the past

11

years that the source of Europe's security problem is the discrepancy between east and west in conventional arms.

If so, some claim, let us demilitarize the Samarian and Judaean hills and if war breaks out we will have enough time to prepare for it. We remind them that it is extremely difficult, under the circumstances confronting Israel, to provide ample warning time against the enemies' intentions. We are dealing with totalitarian regimes which make far-reaching decisions by a few people, under great secrecy. Despite Israel's excellent intelligence, one of the best in the world, major intelligence failures under Middle East conditions must be taken into account. In addition, it must be remembered that we are faced with huge standing armies, able to remain a long time in a readiness of several hours, whereas the State of Israel will always have a very small standing army and it would take a number of days to mobilize its reserves, especially in light of the introduction of surface-to-surface missiles at the disposal of enemy armies.

The test of need leads to a clear conclusion: there is no possibility of ensuring Israel's national security without complete control of Samaria and Judaea. In other words, without these parts of our homeland we are unable to retain the State of Israel as a safe haven for the Jewish people.

THE SECOND TEST: 'CAN THE PEOPLE, FROM WHOSE POSSESSION YOU CLAIM A PORTION, SPARE THAT PORTION?'

In his book, *The Jewish War Front*, Jabotinsky wrote in 1940:

There is only one circumstance in which it is a tragedy to constitute a minority: it is the case of the people which is minority, everywhere and always only a minority, dispersed among alien races with no corner of the earth to call its own, and no home in which to find refuge. Such is not the position of the Arabs, with four Arab countries on the east of the Suez Canal, and five others west of Suez. Some of these countries are already independent, others are not so as yet; but in each of them there is no question of any but an Arab majority; each of them is already an Arab national homeland.

Two generations have passed since those words were written. Not nine but 21 Arab nations have achieved independence, all of them members of the Arab League, each a 'national Arab homeland'. Let us not forget that the demand to establish the twenty-second Arab state, in Western Eretz Yisrael, was raised by the PLO as early as 1964 when Samaria, Judaea and the Gaza district were in Arab hands and Israel was bounded between the 'green line' and the sea. The timing of that demand and the tactics employed by the PLO to achieve it are proof of the demanders' true intent, yet even they resort to verbal acrobatics to justify themselves: The first paragraph of the Palestinian Covenant states that 'Palestine is the homeland of the Arab Palestinian people; it is an indivisible part of the Arab homeland, and the Palestinian people are an integral part of the Arab nation.' The Arab nation has enjoyed the fullest possible expression of its right to self-determination through the establishment of independent states. The Arab nation has no right to establish, west of the Jordan River, another Arab state, the twenty-second. This position is given extra validity by the fact that those who desire to establish the twenty-second Arab state intend to destroy the State of Israel.

According to the reality of this region, we must clearly state: it is an either/or situation. Either Israel controls Samaria, Judaea and the Gaza district, or a murderous terrorist state will be set up there, headed by some faction of the PLO or Hamas. The Hashemite kingdom has no chance of holding on to these areas, and if it receives them from us it will be able to control them for only a short period of time. A combination of terrorism, rioting with intra-Arab and inter-

13

national pressures would force the Hashemites to pull out of Western Eretz Yisrael quickly. In any case, the idea of 'territorial compromise' with the Hashemite kingdom – relinquishing parts of Samaria, Judaea and maybe the Gaza district, and extending Israeli sovereignty over the remaining parts of Western Eretz Yisrael – has been removed from the diplomatic agenda after King Hussein's announcement last summer that he is severing his country's ties with the area west of the Jordan.

The conclusion drawn from the second test is therefore clear. The fact that we are blocking the establishment of a new Arab state in Western Eretz Yisrael does not cause any wrong. Being aware of its purposes, we can safely say that the prevention of the establishment of a terror state between Iraq, Syria and Libya is an act of justice.

THE THIRD TEST: 'HISTORICAL RIGHTS IN SUPPORT OF THE CLAIM TO A DEFINITE PIECE OF TERRITORY'

Forty-one years after its establishment it seems that we must reiterate that our State was conceived, as we find in the Declaration of Independence, as 'a Jewish state in Eretz Yisrael' and this, as it says there, 'by virtue of our natural and historic right'.

The borders of the state were not outlined at its inception, and this was not a coincidence; the ceasefire line demarcated in 1949, and drawn in maps as the 'green line' was nothing but the 'Line-of-Battle-Fatigue', a random line basically reflecting force, and lacking any historical, international or moral validity.

The celebrated declaration that the State of Israel is a Jewish State was practically validated by the Israeli Knesset through the legislation of the Law of Return. The declaration that the Jewish State was established on the grounds of the

14

natural and historical rights of the Jewish people to Eretz Yisrael, was given practical validity by the Knesset in 1967 in the Law and Administration Ordinance, according to which 'the law, jurisdiction and administration of the State shall apply to any area of Eretz Yisrael designated by the government by decree'. This law, passed in the Knesset by an overwhelming majority, does not stipulate any limitations. The application of state sovereignty over any part of Eretz Yisrael is not conditional, according to Israeli law, on Israeli–Arab agreement or on the permission of international institutions. In legal terms this might have been a small step – in Zionism it is certainly a large one.

This triple test, suggested by Ze'ev Jabotinsky, to scrutinize the morality of the realization of the Zionist dream, is a stringent and a fair one. By translating it into today's reality, the conclusion is clear and should be taught to all: our right to Eretz Yisrael is inseparably interwoven with our right to national security. It is therefore necessary for us to apply our rights to this land. In the words that are by now some 70 years old: 'Such, I think, is the ethical aspect of our claim.'

Ha'una, May 1988

A Perennial Stream

SOME 15 YEARS ago I started a research project in which I applied a mathematical equation, known as the 'Heat Equation', to the prediction of the erosion activity of streams in response to changes in elevation at their mouth. This was a new topic for me, and I was surprised to find how little agreement there was between researchers in this field. I therefore mentioned, in the introduction to the research report, words published at that time by Cook and Reeves in their book on desert streams: 'A reader of the prodigious arroyo literature may be justifiably perplexed by the shifting currents of conflicting arguments, the discharge of unsubstantiated assertions, the pools of controversy, and the shoals of abandoned hypotheses.'

Fifty years after the death of Ze'ev Jabotinsky it appears that among the factions of the Zionist movement, Revisionist Zionism is to be considered a perennial stream, direct and consistent. The doctrine at the base of this political school of thought is a 'strong theory' that stands up to the revolutions of Time and Man. The man who formulated this doctrine, the chief spokesman of this organization was, and in many ways remains, Ze'ev Jabotinsky. Unintentionally, Jabotinsky disclosed one of the basic secrets of the strength of his approach in an answer to the ironic question asked by Lord Peel, in the course of his testimony before his committee in London, in 1937:

Lord Peel: You think you have the brains really?
Mr Jabotinsky: It is a great question whether it requires more 'brains' to be straightforward than not to be straightforward. I do not know. It is a 'moot' point, as I think you call it in English.

16

It may be that this is an important difference between the Zionist Revisionist trend – explicit and direct – and the other Zionist trends, which meander and even retreat as they flow forward. We can check this assertion with the help of a few examples from Zionist history, not for the sake of overdue polemics but in order to learn a lesson for the present and future.

* * *

In the 1920s, one of the fiercest arguments in the Zionist movement revolved around the issue of the relation to the Arabs. The Socialist Zionists nurtured delusions derived from their social views, and one of their important representatives, David Ben-Gurion, said at the Fourth Congress of Achduth Ha'avoda (the United Labour) at Ein Harod in 1924:

Let us not be afraid to admit publicly that between ourselves, the Jewish workers, and the leadership of the Arab movement today, between the Effendi, there is no common language. The Effendi see us not only as national opponents, but mainly as a class enemy . . . There is no common platform between ourselves and the ruling class of the Arab nation. However, there is a common platform between us and the Arab workers, although not existing practically – but potentially. The Arab worker does not exist as a force or political factor standing for himself. Multitudes of workers, mainly the Fallaheens, are illiterate. They are immersed in ignorance. They are pressured and oppressed by the landowners, profiteers and money-lenders. The Arab worker is unorganized, lacking class awareness – but this situation will change – and we will play a decisive part in this change.

A few years later Ben-Gurion became disillusioned, and wrote of his discussions with Arab leaders:

At the 18th Congress [1933] I was elected, along with Moshe Sharett and Eliezer Kaplan, to the Zionist Executive, and I decided to take practical steps to bring about an agreement with the Arabs. The assumption then accepted within the Zionist movement was that we constitute a blessing for the Arabs in the country, and that therefore they have no basis to oppose us. In my initial meeting with Musa Alami along with M. Sharett (which took place in Sharett's home, as there was then no apartment in Jerusalem) this assumption was shaken. When Musa Alami told me: 'I would rather this land be poor and barren even another hundred years until we Arabs become talented enough to make it flourish and develop', I felt that as an Arab patriot he had the right to say it.

However, already ten years beforehand, in 1923, Ze'ev Jabotinsky formulated the most accurate and realistic summary of the Jewish-Arab problem, a summary that is valid to this very day, in his well-known article 'About the Iron Wall':

This does not mean that there cannot be any agreement with the Palestine Arabs. What is impossible is a voluntary agreement. As long as the Arabs feel that there is the least hope of getting rid of us, they will refuse to give up this hope in return for either kind words or for bread and butter, because they are not a rabble, but a living people. And when a living people yields in matters of such a vital character it is only when there is no longer any hope of getting rid of us, because they can make no breach in the iron wall. Not till then will they drop their extremist leaders whose watchword is 'Never!' And the leadership will pass to the moderate groups, who will approach us with a proposal that we should both agree to mutual concessions. Then we may expect them to discuss honestly practical questions, such as a guarantee against Arab displacement, or equal rights for Arab citizens, or Arab national integrity.

And when that happens, I am convinced that we Jews will be found ready to give them satisfactory guarantees, so that both peoples can live together in peace, like good neighbours. But the only way to obtain such an agreement is the iron wall, which is to say a strong power in Palestine that is not amenable to any Arab pressure. In other words, the only way to reach an agreement in the future is to abandon all idea of seeking an agreement in the present.

* * *

In the 1930s, there took place the heated dispute within the Zionist movement as to the formulation of the ultimate goal of Zionism. An indirect confrontation on this issue occurred in the Peel Commission, before which in Jerusalem in January 1937 the senior representative of the Jewish Agency, David Ben-Gurion, testified:

We did not say to make in Palestine a Jewish State. We did not say it at that time and we do not say it now and I will tell you why. There are three reasons ... A state may imply – since there are two nationalities – domination of others, the domination by the Jewish majority of the minority, but that is not our aim.

Lord Peel: That is why you want a Mandate, to keep you out of temptation?

Mr Ben-Gurion: No. We said that before there was question of a Mandate; it was before the war, in 1897 ... The second reason is that a state means a separate political entity ... and we should like this country to be attached to a greater unit, a unit that is called the British Commonwealth of Nations.

There is a third reason why we do not use the formula of a Jewish State. There are holy places in Palestine which are holy to the whole civilized world and we are unwilling and it is not in our interest that we should be made responsible for them ... There is no difference between a National Home for the Jewish people and what is ordinarily meant by a Jewish State, except that there is one advantage in a National Home. Why? A Jewish State, as in the case of any other state, would mean the sovereignty of the people of that state at any given time. They may decide without giving any reasons who shall or shall not come into that state. The Palestinian Jews, however numerous they may be and however they may by virtue of their numbers dominate the country, have no right to refuse to admit other Jews as long as there is a place in this country. A National Home for the Jewish people is, in that respect, a much larger conception than a Jewish State.

Commission member, Sir Horace Rumbold: You mean there might come a moment when, if there was a Jewish National State, they might say 'We have enough people here, we do not want any more of you'?

Mr Ben-Gurion: Yes, without giving any reason for it, but they cannot do it, when there is a National Home for the Jewish people.

* * *

19

Such were the words of a senior representative of the Zionist Movement in the Jerusalem winter of 1937. Ze'ev Jabotinsky was denied entrance to Eretz Yisrael and therefore he testified before the Peel Commission at its meeting in London, on 22 February 1937, saying:

The phenomenon called Zionism may include all kinds of dreams – a 'model community', Hebrew culture, perhaps even a second edition of the Bible – but all this longing for wonderful toys of velvet and silver is nothing in comparison with that tangible momentum of irresistible distress and need by which we are propelled and borne . . . Yes. We do want a State; every nation on earth, every normal nation, beginning with the smallest and the humblest, who do not claim any merit, any role in humanity's development, they all have States of their own.

. . . I am going to make a 'terrible' confession. Our demand for a Jewish majority is not our maximum; it is our minimum; it is just an inevitable stage if only we are allowed to go on salvaging our people. The point when the Jews will reach in that country a majority will not be the point of saturation yet, because with 1,000,000 more Jews in Palestine today you could already have a Jewish majority, but there are certainly 3,000,000 or 4,000,000 in the East who are virtually knocking at the door asking for admission, which means for salvation.

Two years before the outbreak of the Second World War, those who were 'knocking at the door' did not enjoy salvation by the British government. In July 1937 the Peel Commission submitted its conclusions and advocated the establishment of a Jewish state on a fifth of Western Eretz Yisrael.

Now Ben-Gurion, in a great twist, turned back his discharge of winter claims and in the summer warmly blessed the Commission's recommendations:

. . . The important thing in the Commission's report, which places it, in my opinion, in line with the Balfour Declaration, if not above it, is the declaration of a Jewish State in Eretz Yisrael. After two thousand years of slavery, dispersion and dependency, an enormous government which controls the country offers us sovereignty in our homeland, political freedom in our land.

Ze'ev Jabotinsky, on the other hand, had no illusions in his reaction to the Peel Commission's decision as he spoke before members of the British Parliament:

On the other hand, both the Royal Commission and the Government clearly encourage the proposed Arab State to join a future Arab Federation, so that the little villa is to be surrounded by a more or less united mass of covetous appetites about ten million strong. I said 'united': they may differ on many things, but they can be confidently expected to agree on this one point, that Neboth's vineyard must be captured.

Strategically, how can this 'Pale' be defended against any serious aggression? Most of it is lowland, whereas the Arab hills are within fifteen miles from Tel-Aviv and twenty miles from Haifa; in a few hours these towns can be destroyed, the harbours made useless, and most of the plains overrun, whatever the valour of their defenders.

*   *   *

The joy of the leaders of the Zionist movement for the idea of a dwarfed Jewish state did not last long, and the destruction of European Jewry forced them to redefine the Zionist goal. In May 1942, with the approval of David Ben-Gurion, the American Zionist Conference demanded at the New York Biltmore Hotel that 'Eretz Yisrael shall become a Jewish community, integrated with the new democratic structure of the world', and after the war ended, the Zionist Conference in London reached the following decision, in August 1945:

Any solution to the double and indivisible issue of the People of Israel and the Land of Israel is inconceivable without the establishment of Eretz Yisrael, undivided and not diminished, as a Hebrew state, in accordance with the intent of the Balfour Declaration.

Any postponement in solving this question, any attempt at a partial or a paper solution which has no true and quick implementation, do not reflect the tragedy situation and may only increase the suffering of the nation and the tension in the country.

Again then, if only for a short while, the river of Zionism

was re-directed toward its goal, 14 precious years after the Zionist Congress rejected Ze'ev Jabotinsky's proposal to declare that the goal of Zionism is the establishment of a Jewish majority in Eretz Yisrael.

Jabotinsky would not accompany the Zionist movement, and would not witness the implementation of the London Conference's decisions into the formation of the Joint Resistance Movement in November 1945. Then for nine months, all Jewish military organizations joined forces, but only until the British reacted with 'Operation Broadside' on Shabbat, 29 June 1946. The next day, the headquarters of the Joint Resistance Movement issued the following proclamation in their leaflet 'The Wall: Security and Defence Matters':

Britain has waged war against the Jewish people! The Jewish people will reply with a stormy battle! The Hebrew revolt will continue! The Hebrew revolt has only begun! The Hebrew underground stands firmly at the Nation's service! Down with the Nazi-British rule! The impure sons of Titus – out of the holy land! Ruined Yagur – we will yet rebuild you and you shall be rebuilt! Long live free immigration! Long live the Jewish State!

Not for long were these exclamations calling the Jewish youth in Eretz Yisrael. In August 1946 the Zionist leadership met in Paris for urgent consultation, and ordered a halt to the military struggle against 'the impure sons of Titus'. It accepted Nachum Goldman's suggestion 'to propose negotiations to establish a viable state in an appropriate part of Eretz Yisrael', and again the flow of Zionism turned back. Nine years earlier they praised the *forced* partition of Eretz Yisrael, but now a partition plan was *initiated* by the official Zionist leadership, and the United Nations adopted the idea of partition a year later, on 2 November 1947. There was dancing in the streets of Eretz Yisrael, but David Ben-Gurion felt, as he wrote, 'a mourner among grooms', as he knew what was to come.

On 14 May 1948 David Ben-Gurion led his companions in the courageous decision to establish the Jewish State, 'on the basis of the natural and historical right of the Jewish nation'. Eleven years earlier, Ze'ev Jabotinsky declared before the Peel Commission, in a loud and clear but lonely voice, that 'every nation on the face of the earth, every normal nation – each has its own state'. Now the circle has been closed, as the Declaration of Independence of the State of Israel established that 'it is the natural right of the Jewish nation to be as all other nations, to stand on its own in its sovereign state'.

* * *

Fifty years after the death of Ze'ev Jabotinsky, his followers rest their policies on the two Zionist pillars as he defined them: the right of the Jewish people to its land, and the need to implement this right, as formulated so well by the Zionist Conference in London, five years after his death.

It is by these principles that we must openly and firmly stand, and the reason for this is both moral and practical: The solution to a complicated problem demands concentrated effort; concentration of effort demands systematic action, and systematic action must be based on consistency, being a result of internal rationale. This is because policies must convince not only those individuals who directly make decisions, but also the general public, who decide indirectly.

In the chapter 'Leader', in his *Memoirs of My Generation*, Ze'ev Jabotinsky wrote:

This was Herzl. He conquered our thoughts, and this was a fact, not an office. In other words, it was Truth. Real leaders are seldom born and often their distinction is that they do not claim to 'Lead'. To obey them is not a question of discipline; they are obeyed in the same manner as we are swayed by a talented singer, for his tune expresses our own longings.

23

And there is yet another sign: A person such as Herzl, when he dies, and thirty years pass, he still remains our leader.

These very words are well-suited to their writer. Indeed, 'it was Truth' and yes, 'there is yet another sign': When he dies, and 50 years pass, he still remains our leader. And time and time again we are carried with his thoughts, which flow as a river, 'Cool and Steadfast'.

Ha'una, August 1990

How difficult is it
to predict the future?

IT HAS BEEN said that 'it is difficult to predict, and especially the future'. Let's examine the validity of this observation.

Seventy years ago, on 4 October 1917, the British War Cabinet discussed the possibility of issuing a declaration favouring the return of the Jews to Eretz Yisrael, also known as Palestine. One of the participants urged objections, as recorded in the minutes:

Lord Curzon [Lord President of the Council] urged strong objections upon practical grounds. He stated, from his recollection of Palestine, that the country was, for the most part, barren and desolate; there being but sparse cultivation on the terraced slopes, the valleys and streams being few, and large centres of population scarce. A less propitious seat for the future Jewish race could not be imagined. How was it proposed to get rid of the existing majority of Mussulman inhabitants and to introduce the Jews in their place? How many would be willing to return and on what pursuits would they engage?

To secure for the Jews already in Palestine equal civil and religious rights seemd to him a better policy than to aim at repatriation on a large scale. He regarded the latter as sentimental idealism, which would never be realised, and that His Majesty's Government should have nothing to do with it.

So, indeed, it is difficult to predict, and especially the future.

On 2 November 1917 Mr Balfour, then the British Secretary of State for Foreign Affairs, sent a letter whose contents became known as the Balfour Declaration, beginning with the words:

Dear Lord Rothschild, I have much pleasure in conveying to you, on behalf of His Majesty's Government, the following declaration of sympathy with the Jewish Zionist aspirations, which has been submitted to and approved of by the Cabinet.

And five years later, it was declared in the Council of the League of Nations assembled in London, on 24 July 1922:

Whereas the Principal Allied Powers have also agreed that the Mandatory should be responsible for putting into effect the declaration originally made on 2 November 1917 by the Government of His Britannic Majesty, and adopted by the said Powers, in favour of the establishment in Palestine of a national home for the Jewish people, recognition has thereby been given to the historical connexion of the Jewish people with Palestine and to the grounds for reconstituting their national home in that country.

It was a great triumph for historic justice.

The idea that the Jewish State should be reconstituted in Eretz Yisrael, the notion that the land of Israel belongs as of right to the Jewish people, found its clear expression in 1948, in the Declaration of the establishment of our State:

We, Members of the People's council, representatives of the Jewish community of Eretz Yisrael and of the Zionist Movement, are here assembled on the day of the termination of the British mandate over Eretz Yisrael, and by virtue of our natural and historic right and on the strength of the resolution of the United Nations General Assembly, hereby declare the establishment of a Jewish State in Eretz Yisrael, to be known as the State of Israel.

No borders were determined by the State of Israel at its inception. After a prolonged war with our Arab neighbours, the tortuous 'Green Line' of armistice was demarcated. It has no historic or moral significance whatsoever – it is nothing but the line of battle fatigue. At any rate, with the Arab aggression in June 1967 it was politically buried, despite recurring attempts on the part of our enemies as well as some friends to revive it.

In the next 25 years the Balfour Declaration would turn into a series of disappointments. One of these was the Palestine Royal Commission, chaired by the Right Honourable Earl Peel, which in 1937 recommended a new partition of Palestine west of the Jordan River.

Almost exactly 50 years ago, on 11 February 1937, a great Zionist, Ze'ev Jabotinsky, testified before the Peel Commission saying:

I am going to make a 'terrible' confession. Our demand for a Jewish majority is not our maximum – it is our minimum, it is just an inevitable stage if only we are allowed to go on salvaging our people. The point when the Jews will reach in that country a majority will not be the point of saturation yet – because with 1,000,000 more Jews in Palestine today you could already have a Jewish majority, but there are certainly 3,000,000 or 4,000,000 in the East who are virtually knocking at the door asking for admission, which means for salvation.

We have known for the last 48 years that it meant exactly that – Salvation with a capital S. Some people, then, *can* predict.

Five months later, after that Royal Commission published its recommendations regarding partition, Ze'ev Jabotinsky addressed Members of Parliament in this very building, saying:

But what the Royal Commission proposes is quite different. On the one hand the Jewish 'State' is to be reduced to this dwarfish proportion – a district so small that its Jewish defenders will always remain a handful. It almost looks like a lonely villa on the seashore: a villa belonging to a rival race, and a villa so poorly protected.

On the other hand, both the Royal Commission and the Government clearly encourage the proposed Arab State to join a future Arab Federation, so that the little villa is to be surrounded by a more or less united mass of covetous appetites about ten million strong. I said 'united': they may differ on many things, but they can be confidently expected to agree on this one point, that Naboth's vineyard must be captured.

Strategically, how can this 'Pale' be defended against any serious

27

aggression? Most of it is lowland, whereas the Arab reserve is all hills. Guns can be placed on the Arab hills within 15 miles of Tel-Aviv and 20 miles of Haifa; in a few hours these towns can be destroyed, the harbours made useless, and most of the plains overrun whatever the valour of their defenders.

Ten years after Jabotinsky's address in this building, Egypt, Saudi Arabia, Iraq, Syria and the Hashemite Kingdom of Jordan, united their covetous appetites in an attempt to smother the baby State of Israel. The result was an unlawful occupation of the Gaza area by Egypt, and an unlawful occupation of Judaea and Samaria by the Hashemites. Up to 6 June 1967 the ten-mile-wide Israel faced a very real threat of being overrun within a few hours, as foreseen by Jabotinsky.

Some people, obviously, can predict, and even the future.

In 1967 we witnessed an attempt at a rerun. Again the rival Arab states united against Israel, with Hussein unable to resist the temptation, to restrain his appetite, joining Syria and Egypt in an attempt to push us into the Mediterranean. However, this time, as a result of repelling this joint aggression, Judaea and Samaria lawfully came under the control of Israel.

Let us note that even those who would like to see Israel ultimately relinquishing Judaea and Samaria to the Hashemite Kingdom of Jordan should remember that resolutions of various United Nations organs calling on Israel to unilaterally withdraw its forces from these areas do not have any basis in international law. Let us also note that even those who view Judaea and Samaria as occupied areas should bear in mind that the Supreme Court of Israel, sitting as a High Court of Justice has assumed jurisdiction over the military commanders in these areas, and that this is the first occasion in the history of military occupation that citizens of an occupied territory have been allowed a direct appeal to the high court of the occupying power.

There is, therefore, nothing unlawful, nothing immoral in Israel's control of Judaea and Samaria. And let me be very specific: There is nothing immoral, despite the opinion that found favour in some quarters, in our total objection to the idea of the establishment of yet another Palestinian Arab state in Judaea and Samaria, namely, a PLO, pro-Soviet terrorist base.

We are sometimes preached to on the basis of the alleged necessity to apply the right of self-determination to the Arab inhabitants of Judaea and Samaria. Sometimes this is coupled with an attempt to convince us that this should be the political solution on practical grounds.

Practical arguments are sometimes called for by some of our friends who try to persuade us that it is not worthwhile for us to keep our control of Judaea and Samaria. To test the validity of these arguments let us play a game: I shall read a part of an editorial which appeared in the prestigious London *Times* of 7 September. It will be your role to guess what is wrong in this quotation.

In that case it might be worthwhile for the Israeli Government to consider whether they should exclude altogether the project, which has found favour in some quarters, of making Israel a more homogeneous State by the secession of that fringe of alien population who are contiguous to the nation with which they are united by race. In any case, the wishes of the population concerned would seem to be a decisively important element in any solution that can hope to be regarded as permanent, and the advantages to Israel of becoming a homogeneous State might conceivably outweigh the obvious disadvantages of losing the Judaea and Samaria districts of the borderland.

The solution to this riddle is simple. The editorial appeared with a change of but a few names, on 7 September 1938, a short while before Chamberlain went to Munich. The Germans interpreted it correctly: it reflected the mood of the British government, which, in addition to pseudo-moral arguments, resorted to pseudo-practical ones in order to twist the Czech arm on the issue of the Sudeten Hills, that strategic buffer zone between Germany and Czechoslovakia. The original reads as follows:

> In that case it might be worthwhile for the Czechoslovak Government to consider whether they should exclude altogether the project, which has found favour in some quarters, of making Czechoslovakia a more homogeneous State by the secession of that fringe of alien populations who are contiguous to the nation with which they are united by race . . . The advantages to Czechoslovakia of becoming a homogeneous State might conceivably outweigh the obvious disadvantages of losing the Sudeten German districts of the borderland.

It is, I believe, an interesting exercise. I propose that the analogy is valid, and I think the moral is useful: do not hasten to advise a friend if he is to bear the harsh consequences of your advice.

We do seek peace with our neighbouring states. The only way to reach peace with our neighbours – anchored in peace treaties – is to conduct direct negotiations, within the framework of the Camp David accords, as stated in the guiding principles of the Government of Israel. But peace must be based on security, otherwise peace is a meaningless word. We must be able to defend such a treaty that we hope to sign. The hills of Judaea and Samaria are a decisive factor in our ability to retain stability in our part of the Middle East.

*   *   *

Elaborating now on the issue of the national will to resist a threat, let us turn to the prelude to war of 1939, namely to the Munich Agreement, in reference to which the British historian, A. J. P. Taylor, wrote in his book *The Origins of the Second World War*:

> British policy over Czechoslovakia originated in the belief that Ger-

many had a moral right to the Sudeten German territory on grounds of national principle; and it drew the further corollary that this victory for self determination would provide a stabler, more permanent peace in Europe ...

... It was triumph for all that was best and most enlightened in British life, a triumph for those who had preached equal justice between peoples ...

... with skill and persistence, Chamberlain brought first the French and then the Czechs to follow the moral line ...

What folly!

William Shirer, in his book *The Dreadful Years*, also described the mood:

'My good friends!' exclaimed Chamberlain on his return from Munich, 'This is the second time in our history that there has come back from Germany to Downing Street peace with honour. I believe it is peace in our time.'

Yes, it is difficult to predict, and especially the future.

The British press, Parliament and the people were jubilant, hailing the returning Prime Minister as a hero. *The Times* wrote that 'no conqueror returning from the battlefield has come adorned with nobler laurels'. Only Duff Cooper, the First Lord of the Admiralty, resigned from the Cabinet in protest. And when in the ensuing House of Commons debate Churchill rose to brand Munich 'as a total, unmitigated defeat', he was forced to pause until a storm of hostile shouting had subsided.

'You were given the choice between war and dishonour,' Churchill said. 'You chose dishonour and you will have war.'

Some people, obviously, can predict, and even the future, but not quite: when Great Britain went to war – bitter, cruel, demanding blood, tears, toil and sweat – the Jewish people went to the slaughterhouse.

It is apparently not too difficult to deceive the moral senses of a civilized person. The Munich case is an extraordinarily

31

useful example of the abuse of the concept of the right to self determination. This concept, as you know, has been abused by the PLO since its establishment in 1964, three years before Judaea and Samaria came under Israeli control in a war of self-defence. This idea cannot be applied to the Arab inhabitants of Judaea, Samaria and the Gaza District, as can be learned even from the PLO charter itself:

Article 1: Palestine is the homeland of the Arab Palestinian people; it is an indivisible part of the Arab homeland, and the Palestinian people are an integral part of the Arab Nation.

The Arab nation enjoys, in the fullest possible way, its right to self-determination. It finds its expression in 21 independent states. No other nation on earth enjoys such an expression of its national aspirations. To play on the linguistic difference between a nation and a people is ridiculous. If this distinction is valid, it would allow the Jews in Brooklyn, New York, to declare the independent Jewish State of Brooklyn, being the 'separate American Jewish People', an 'integral part' of the Jewish nation. This is a cynical attempt to exploit the good will and naive approach of citizens of the free world. Fifty years after Munich, no decent person with eyes in his head should fall into the political trap of the alleged Palestinian Arabs' right to self-determination. To be blunt – as sometimes bluntness is needed – it is a bluff.

The 'Final Political Statement of the Fourth Convention of the Fatah Organization', issued in Damascus on 31 May 1980 stated in Article 8 that the aim of the Fatah movement is 'the liquidation of the Zionist entity – politically, economically, militarily, culturally and ideologically' and that 'the establishment of a democratic Palestinian state on all of the Palestinian land will assure the legitimate rights of all its inhabitants and it will be able to actively participate in the realization of the goals of the Arab nation in the liberation of its countries and the establishment of a united progressive Arab society'.

The infamous Palestinian Covenant, the PLO charter, issued in 1964, states in its Article 19 that the establishment of the State of Israel is 'entirely illegal, regardless of the passage of time'. Article 20 says: 'The Balfour Declaration, the Mandate for Palestine and everything that has been based upon them, are deemed null and void'. Article 22 states: 'The liberation of Palestine will destroy the Zionist and imperialist presence . . .'.

In other words, this is an excuse for terrorism, and a poor one. In his article, 'The Cancer of Terrorism', Paul Johnson wrote last year:

Modern terrorism dates from the middle 1960s, when the PLO formally adopted terror and mass murder as its primary policy. Terrorism was thus able to draw on the immense financial resources of the Arab oil states, and on the military training programmes of the Soviet Union and of its satellites . . . It acquired the weaponry of a sizeable modern army and set up terrorist training camps of its own, used as facilities by the Red Brigades, the IRA, and a score of other killer gangs throughout the world.

In capsule: the PLO raises rootless political claims and uses ruthless terrorist methods. It must not be allowed to establish a radical, pro-Soviet terrorist state between Libya and Syria.

Convinced that a PLO state is an impossibility, some people believe that the idea of a territorial compromise holds some promise.

Allow me to dampen any enthusiasm in this respect. I propose that it is naive and unrealistic to expect that King Hussein will be either willing or able to sign an agreement based on territorial compromise. The reason is simple: a territorial compromise, from his point of view, means that Jordan would gain control of most of Judaea, Samaria or Gaza, but some of the area would be retained by Israel. For him it

33

would mean that he is asked to sign a document proclaiming that he, the Hashemite Arab King, agrees to transfer parts of 'sacred Arab land' to the Jewish nation for posterity. No Arab leader, in the foreseeable future, would sign such a document.

But even those who favoured the idea in 1967 must consider some changes in vital strategic military statistics, namely the Order of Battle east of the Jordan River. In 1967, in four countries, all of which have participated in wars against Israel – Syria, Jordan, Saudi Arabia and Iraq – the conventional arms military capacity on our eastern front included 1100 tanks, 370 combat aircraft and 190,000 soldiers. Today the following arsenal can be deployed against us by the same countries: almost 11,000 tanks, 1600 combat aircraft, 7000 artillery pieces, 1,200,000 soldiers and 13,000 armoured personnel carriers.

These are a lot of lethal toys. For the sake of comparison, take NATO: In order to contain a Soviet attack on Western Europe, some 23,000 tanks are employed by NATO forces. That is, the eastern Arab coalition has acquired half of NATO's power, and we may have to contain them in a stretch of land 50 miles wide. Shrunk back into the pre-1967 lines, where Israel was about ten miles wide, this would become a 'mission impossible'.

But maybe these are only harmless toys? Maybe the Arabs do not intend to use them against the Jewish State? A partial answer can be found in the words of the Iraqi despot, Saddam Hussein, who was quoted in the Kuwaiti newspaper *Al-Anaba* on 19 January 1980 as saying:

Thirty kilometres are enough in order to break the back of Israel. A number of kilometres are enough so that Israel will collapse. The Camp David agreements are rejected; we are ready to accept a solution that will restore to the Arabs and to Iraq full rights in Palestine without shedding blood. The solution is that Palestine will be returned to the Arabs and the Arabs will return to Palestine – all of Palestine.

The combination of these rhetorics and the formidable military machines is, indeed, dynamite.

* * *

Recognition of the moral basis of our Zionist concept is of utmost importance. In a way, it can be judged on the backdrop of what Prime Minister Thatcher told a joint session of the United States Congress in February 1985:

Wars are not caused by the buildup of weapons. They are caused when an aggressor believes he can achieve his objectives at an acceptable price. The war of 1939 was not caused by an arms race. It sprang from a tyrant's belief that other countries lacked the means and the will to resist him.

Therefore it must be concluded that without Israel's control of the hilly country of Judaea and Samaria one cannot expect stability in our part of the Middle East, and in such a case a peace agreement will not be defendable, that is, it will be worthless.

A sound policy toward Judaea and Samaria rests on two pillars: the natural, historical right of the Jewish people to the Land of Israel, and the vital necessity to fully exercise this right in order to maintain long-term, reasonable national security. And since to this policy, albeit difficult, there simply is no moral, logical alternative – this is the road we must, and will, pursue.

Speech before members of the British Parliament, London, May 1987

The Importance of Drawing Conclusions

I WOULD LIKE to speak about the importance of drawing conclusions in politics. Politics is sometimes referred to as 'the art of the possible'. But I'd like to take issue with that definition; since it has to do with the possible, it cannot be an art. It is a craft. We need some craftsmen, we need politicians, some of them are good at their job, but they are only able to stay afloat, not to head towards new directions. The political art is rightly called statesmanship. I'd like to suggest that in this century, at least for the Jewish people, we cannot afford a diet of politics alone. We need statesmanship in the sense of progress towards new goals, and the characteristics of statesmanship from this point of view are three: the ability to observe, the will to draw conclusions, and the skill to move ahead. Now, drawing conclusions might be the difficult part of the three components. This was noticed already in 1930 by the mentor of this movement, Ze'ev Jabotinsky, who said that 'having a mood and making a decision are two different things'. And he even contemplated for a while that people who are willing to draw conclusions are of a different breed altogether.

In 1930 he related the following:

One of my friends, whose position on Zionist issues is rather remote from mine, conveyed, after the bloody riots of last year [1929 in Eretz Israel], an enthusiastic speech which I liked. I told him, Well then, why don't you draw conclusions from your own words? He pondered and answered me slowly, quietly, with the face of a man about to reveal his

36

most sacred feelings: There is no need to draw conclusions. In general I object to the drawing of conclusions.

So it may be a wholly different breed. Ze'ev Jabotinsky himself was of course both a keen observer and a very bold drawer of conclusions.

In May 1939, just four or five months before the German march on Poland, Jabotinsky addressed the Jews in Poland. In one of his speeches he said:

Even despair may be considered a reaction, but what I see among the multitudes of Jews in eastern Europe is worse. There's indifference, fatalism, people behave as if they have been already sentenced. I have not seen anything like that in history. Even in novels I have not read of such a surrender to fate. What is it like? It is as if people have been put in a wagon, 12 million learned and experienced people, put in a wagon which is pushed to the edge of a canyon. I'm coming to you for an attempt, a last attempt. I call upon you, put an end to this situation, try to halt the wagon, try to jump out of it, try to put some obstacles in its way. Do not go like sheep to the wolf. When the wolf eats one sheep and then two, the others are scared, they shiver and run, but here – one big cemetery.

And so it was, all over Europe, from the Baltic to the Black Sea.

This man, who devoted his life to the establishment of an independent Jewish State in the Land of Israel as a permanent haven for the Jews, was sometimes considered to be a dreamer, a person out of touch with reality. But when you read his writings today, you realize that he was indeed a very shrewd person with a very practical approach to world affairs, who showed a very keen understanding of the realities of the Middle East.

In 1937 Jabotinsky fought against the idea of the second partition of the Land of Israel (the first partition took place in 1922 when Eastern Jordan was torn from the western part of Eretz Israel). The memorandum ends:

... strategically, how can this 'Pale' be defended against any serious aggression? Most of it is lowland, whereas the Arab reserve is all hills. Guns can be placed on the Arab hills within 15 miles of Tel Aviv and 20 miles of Haifa. In a few hours these towns can be destroyed, the harbours made useless and most of the plains overrun, whatever the valour of their defenders.

Thirty years later, in June 1967, the United States Secretary of Defense asked the Joint Chiefs of Staff for their views on the 'minimum territory in addition to that held on June 4, '67, Israel might be justified in retaining in order to permit a more effective defense against possible conventional Arab attack and terrorist raids'. And on 29 June, the Joint Chiefs answered in a memorandum signed by Earl G. Wheeler which was declassified about a year ago (and I can only make some guesses as to why it was held classified for all these years):

Threat – the high ground running north–south through the middle of west Jordan overlooks Israel's narrow mid-section and offers a route for a thrust to the sea which would split the country into two parts. Requirements – a boundary along the commanding terrain overlooking the Jordan River from the west could provide a shorter defense line. However, as a minimum, Israel would need a defense line generally along the axis Bardala–Tubas–Nablus–Bira–Jerusalem and then to the northern part of the Dead Sea.

Now, that line recommended by the Joint Chiefs of this mighty country, runs from Nablus to Bira and Jerusalem. This is indeed the backbone of Judaea and Samaria. As a geologist, I might also add that this is the line along the water divide of the western part of Eretz Yisrael. But what are Nablus and Bira? Nablus is the Arab way of pronouncing the Latin name, 'Nea-Polis', the New City, which was established by the Romans 2000 years ago on the ruins of the ancient Shechem. And what is Bira? Bira is about ten miles north of Jerusalem. It is only three miles south of the ancient town of

Beth-el which in Hebrew means Home-of-God. The chapter of the Torah that we read last week is Lech-Lecha, in which, in Genesis 12, we read:

Now the Lord said to Abraham, go from your country and your kindred and your father's house to a land that I will show you ... So Abraham went as the Lord told him ... And they went forth to the land of Canaan. When they had come to the land of Canaan, Abraham passed through the land to the place of Shechem ... Then the Lord appeared to Abraham and said: 'To your descendants I will give this land'. So he built there an altar to the Lord. Then he moved to the mountain on the east of Beth-el and pitched his tent and there he built an altar to the Lord. And Abraham journeyed on still going towards the Negev.

Let us just for the moment ponder about this in a purely objective and intellectual way. Isn't this interesting, so to speak, that in a span of time of 3600 years, with all the developments of modern sophisticated weaponry, including ballistic missiles, the American Joint Chiefs came to the same conclusions as this Patriarch, who was also a great warrior? He understood that in order to secure the life of a nation in this part of the world on a long-term basis, you need to control that 'commanding terrain' in military jargon, that line of 'Bardala–Tubas–Nablus–Bira–Jerusalem'. And since we all know that the military like abbreviations, this string of words can be abbreviated simply to 'Judaea and Samaria'.

But I have not brought out this similarity as a pure intellectual exercise. I have done so because what you have here in a nutshell, are the two moral pillars of our case, fully integrated: on the one hand, our historical, undeniable, natural, inalienable – thereby eternal – right for the Land of Israel, and on the other hand, the vital necessity to implement that right, the urgent need to fully exercise that right in Judaea and Samaria and the Gaza district. Our national security policy in Judaea and Samaria is based on these two

39

moral foundations. And the conclusion to be drawn from that is very clear: we should, as quickly as possible, eliminate the Jewish vacuum that was there in these areas for so long a time. In more positive terms, we must enhance Jewish presence in Judaea and Samaria and the Gaza District, and the practical conclusion from these conclusions is that we must indeed establish Jewish settlements in these areas.

But then they say: 'Well, we can see the logic, but if you push your logic too hard, this will be detrimental to peace'. We should all know, of course, that the contrary is true, that he who assumes that you can buy peace by trading off this little country, Judaea and Samaria, is dead wrong. If he is able to implement this folly, he might be proven to be deadly wrong.

Exactly two years ago, on 11 November 1982, President Reagan, in a different context, said: 'Peace is a product of strength, not of weakness. Of facing reality and not believing in false hopes'.

The idea that you can have stability or peace in our part of the Middle East facing these enormous arsenals on our east and north is simply an illusion, because if Israel is shrunk back to its pre-1967 borders, that very fact will constitute a permanent temptation for that 'thrust' the Joint Chiefs spoke about in their memorandum to the Secretary of Defense. As a proof that this could be a permanent temptation indeed, I'd like to quote Saddam Hussein, the tyrant, the cruel ruler of Iraq, who in January 1980 said, in Arabic of course, to the Kuwait newspaper, *El Anaba*: 'The Camp David agreements are rejected ... The solution is that Palestine will be returned to the Arabs and the Arabs will return to Palestine, all of Palestine. Thirty kilometres are enough to break the back of Israel. A number of kilometres are enough so that Israel will collapse'. He said that in the context of explaining why he was not that successful with his war against Iran but he drew a difference. Here is a vast territory to cross but there it is only 30 kilometres. Now, imagine if he had only 10 miles, as we had before 1967, before the War of Six Days, what kind of temptation that would have constituted? No chance at all for peace and stability.

The conclusion is that not only Jewish settlements are not obstacles to peace but that ultimately they promote stability, and in the future they will secure peace in our part of the Middle East.

To those who say: 'Well, maybe there's something logical in your conclusions, but an increased Jewish presence in Judaea and Samaria and the Gaza District is incompatible with the Camp David accords', I'd like to say again: 'No, this is wrong'. This is neither the time nor the place to have a detailed seminar on Camp David, although I think it is due because it is already six years since the accord was signed and I guess that a few people have really forgotten what it is all about. We don't have the time for details, so I'd like to dwell for a minute on the essence of the accords.

The essence is the establishment of autonomous institutions in Judaea, Samaria and the Gaza District, for a *transitional period* and then, I read from the accord, 'as soon as possible, but not later than the third year after the beginning of this transitional period, negotiations will take place to determine the final status of the West Bank and Gaza'. So we have to expect these negotiations on the final status.

Now, if we had refrained from establishing these settlements, the final status of Judaea and Samaria would have been pre-determined in 1967, simply by default. Because when it came to the table for negotiations, the only realistic solution could have been, God forbid, a pro-Soviet radical state in Judaea and Samaria, maybe disguised for a short transitional period by the rule of the Hashemites. But the real negotiations on the final status of Judaea and Samaria according to

41

Camp David, must entail, at least on equal footing, our claim to these areas. Therefore, establishing settlements and enhancing Jewish presence in Judaea and Samaria is totally compatible with the Camp David accords. On the contrary, I regretfully have to say that deviations from the Camp David accord stem from Washington, not from Jerusalem.

I would have liked to dwell on the details of these deviations but I can stress only one point which has to do with fairness. In the latest presidential campaign, both candidates very eloquently made the point that fairness and morality in public life are badly needed. I would concur with these statements, of course, but in this context, everyone should remember that at Camp David, Maryland, Israel agreed to trade the tangibles for the intangibles. It would be extremely unfair to come now, after Israel has delivered, and say: 'Well, it doesn't really work the way we thought it would and we should change the terms a little'. That's not the way. That's not fairness. That's not morality in public life. We must adhere to the Camp David accords in both spirit and letter and in accordance with the commitment made by the highest authorities of this Administration, namely 'in keeping with Camp David, the US will not be a party to any negotiations of final status issues until the transitional period is under way'. A logical conclusion from that commitment is that you really should not negotiate – even with Israel – issues of final status before the transitional period is under way. Let us negotiate the autonomy and let us defer the other issues, because if you go up hill and put the cart before the horse, you might find yourself sliding down the slope.

I think that on this agenda we might find a lot of support in this country. We need the broadest coalition possible, of Jews and non-Jews alike, on the cause of Israel. I realize that sometimes there are problems in forging such a coalition, but these problems should not hinder us from striving to form the broadest possible coalition of all sources for the cause of the security and well-being of the State of Israel.

The founder of modern Zionism, Theodore Herzel, died 80 years ago, and 50 years ago, Ze'ev Jobotinsky wrote of Herzel's leadership:

Herzel captured our minds. It was a fact, not an office. In other words, it was truth. True leaders are seldom born and sometimes they are recognized through the characteristic that they do not raise any claim to lead. Their leadership is not a question of discipline. We submit to them in the same way we are captured by the singing of a talented singer, because his song is an expression of our own longings. And there is yet another characteristic: a person like Herzel, when he dies and 30 years elapse, he is still our leader.

These words would equally apply to their writer, more than 40 years after he left us. And thus, enlightened by great Zionist statesmen, we shall strive to secure our country, so that in the future, a not very remote future, people will no longer be amazed by the fact that we survive. They will no longer be astonished by the fact that we make it, against all odds, and they will be able to observe quietly, coolly, matter of factly and without any defiance, that yes indeed, Am Yisrael Chai.

Speech to the Herut Movement US Convention, New York, 11 October 1984.

Fifty Years Ago

IN *THE TIMES* of London one September day, there appeared
the following editorial:

If the Arabs now ask for more than the government of Israel is
apparently ready to give in the latest set of proposals, it can only be
inferred that the Arabs are going beyond the mere removal of dis-
abilities and do not find themselves at ease within the State of Israel.

It might be worthwhile for the Israeli government to consider
whether they should exclude altogether the project, which has found
favour in some quarters, of making Israel a more homogeneous state
by the secession of that fringe of alien population who are contiguous
to the nation with which they are united by race.

In any case, the wishes of the population concerned would seem to be
a decisively important element in any solution that can be hoped to be
regarded as permanent, and the advantages to Israel of becoming a
homogeneous state might conceivably outweigh the obvious disadvantages of losing the Judaea and Samaria districts of the border land.

Sharp-eyed readers will already have detected that I have
allowed myself to make certain changes to the text. In the
original article, which was published in *The Times* of London
on 7 September 1938, the word 'Arabs' did not appear, but
'Sudetens', not 'Israel' but 'Czechoslovakia', and not 'Judaea
and Samaria' but 'German Sudeten'. But these, I assure you,
are the only changes I have made in the English text.

The famous editorial of *The Times*, written under the
influence of the British government at the beginning of
September 1938, gave a clear indication to the Germans that
Prime Minister Neville Chamberlain's intention was to reach
an agreement with them on their terms. Indeed, the recom-

44

mendation to create a 'homogeneous state' was confirmed within three weeks at Munich.

Fifty years ago, on 29 September 1938, at 12:30 p.m., the leaders of Italy, France and Britain met Adolf Hitler at Munich. Three days later, in a letter to his sisters, Chamberlain described his impressions of their host: 'When I saw him, his appearance and conduct gave evidence of a storm, despite the fact that he shook my hand with the double handshake that he reserved as an indication of special friendship. However, the signs were misleading. When we began our conversation, his opening sentences were so moderate and reasonable that I felt instant relief.'

In this relaxed atmosphere agreement was reached quickly, and the memorandum was signed at two o'clock on the morning of 30 September 1938. The Czechs were obliged to evacuate the Sudeten mountains in five stages over 10 days, beginning on 1 October. An international committee was to determine the final borders.

Incomprehensible self-delusion and unforgivable cynicism combined to defeat Czechoslovakia, to satisfy temporarily the appetite of the Germans.

While the statesmen waited for the experts to polish the draft of the agreement, Chamberlain, at his request, met Hitler in his Munich apartment on the morning of 30 September and asked him to sign a statement which he had prepared:

We, the Fuehrer and Chancellor of Germany and the Prime Minister of Great Britain . . . are firm in our resolve to adopt the method whereby we shall deal with every other question that may arise between our two countries, and to continue our efforts to remove every possible source of discord, and thus contribute to ensuring the peace of Europe.

Hitler signed, of course.

Upon his return to England, Chamberlain read this empty

statement before the notables who awaited him at the airport. From there he proceeded to London, and outside his residence at 10 Downing Street, announced shortly thereafter before a cheering crowd that he had brought 'peace with honour' and that he 'believed that there would be peace in our time'. However, in the car taking him from the airport, he said to Halifax, the Foreign Secretary, who sat next to him: 'All this will be over within three months.'

It was an only slightly pessimistic guess – 'this' was over within five months. On 20 November 1938 the international committee decided to oblige the Czechs to turn over to the Germans the fortified areas of Sudetenland which defended the Czech democracy against the territorial rapacity of the Germans. Subsequently, the President of Czechoslovakia and its Foreign Minister were forced to sign a statement in Berlin on 15 March 1939 whereby the 'fate of the people and land of Czechoslovakia are placed for safekeeping in the hands of the Leader of the German Reich . . .'

Czechoslovakia's fate was sealed by the statesmen of Europe, but at the basis of their action was their ability to convince their peoples that their policy was not only logical but moral as well.

The excuse to break up Czechoslovakia was supplied by the misuse of the principle of self-determination which Hitler invoked on behalf of the Sudeten Germans. Concerning those who were misled by the false claim, the British historian Taylor wrote with a touch of irony:

British policy over Czechoslovakia originated in the beliefs that Germany had a moral right to the Sudeten German territory on grounds of national principle; and drew the further corollary that this victory for self determination would provide a stabler, more permanent peace in Europe . . . It was a triumph for all that was best and most enlightened in British life, a triumph for those who preach equal justice between people . . . With skill and persistence, Chamberlain brought first the French and then the Czechs to follow the moral line.

It is so easy to be deceived, so pleasant!

Not all analogies, I know, are true, and yet ...

As I write these words 50 years later in Jerusalem, is it really only a light autumn breeze that sends shivers down my spine?

Ma'ariv and *The Boston Globe*, September 1988

Jerusalem, Babylon and New York

I WOULD LIKE to examine the assumption that there must be more than one spiritual centre for the Jewish people. I fail to find the logic in this argument which is based on a rather distorted premise. The reasoning goes something like this: the fact that things are as they are proves that they must be so. According to my scientific training, I find no logic here. The natural state of things – and this is correct with regard to all the nations of the world – is that a nation, or at least the majority of the nation, lives in its own land. In order to convince me that the reverse is desirable, one must adduce weighty reasons, and to this day I have not heard any.

When I hear such an argument, I can almost imagine us in the year 70 CE, almost 2000 years ago. I wonder, did our ancestors ask whether it was desirable that there should be one centre, or various centres? It is well known that there was a spiritual centre in Babylon, and today we hear analogies between that centre and a Jewish centre in the United States. But was the centre in Babylon born out of choice? Did the people say to themselves, 'yes, there is a Jewish centre in Eretz Israel; but Jews have such an important mission among the nations that we should establish such centres in the Diaspora, to the glory of the Jewish people and the glory of the world'?

Surely that is not the case; there was no such choice between Zion on the one hand and the Diaspora on the other. These things were forced upon us from the outside. The question, of course, is whether we have to reconcile ourselves to historical phenomena that were imposed upon us by others.

There are those who argue that the very existence of an important Jewish spiritual centre in the Diaspora proves that Jewish life can be lived outside of Israel, but this is not the case. What does the existence of a Jewish diaspora prove – even when the diaspora is capable of providing educators and intellectuals who think and hope that they are perpetuating the continuity of the Jewish people in the Diaspora? The existence of such a *galut* proves only two things.

First, it proves that the spiritual energy that the Jewish people carried with it on leaving Eretz Israel was so enormous that it sustained Jewish continuity for almost 2000 years despite oppression and persecution. But this does not guarantee that it is possible to store up and draw nourishment from that mighty spiritual energy for many additional years.

Second, in direct opposition to the intention of those authors who are trying to prove that existential reality is the most desirable situation, from the perspective of history it is apparent that there was no resurgence of Jewish life during the last 2000 years that was not almost wholly directed towards Eretz Israel. Were it not for the constant yearning for Eretz Israel, were it not for that feeling of 'My heart is in the East, but I am at the furthermost reaches of the West' (Yehuda Halevi), it would have been impossible to maintain Jewish life in the West.

What are those who seek to prove that contemporary Jewish reality is desirable really arguing? They are proposing to undertake, on the basis of the present situation, the following social experiment: let us continue to draw upon the spiritual energy with which we equipped ourselves some 2000 years ago, and let us abandon the centrality of the Jewish people in Eretz Israel; and let us see what will happen in another 100 or 200 years.

In my humble and non-sociological opinion, such an experiment is a luxury that the Jewish people can ill afford. We must ask ourselves what prospects there are for such an experiment to succeed. Whoever suggests such an experiment takes upon himself a very heavy responsibility towards the Jewish people. The figures concerning assimilation are very simple.

From group responsibility I would like now to turn to personal responsibility. Occasionally an adult, let us say a parent with a young family, tells me: 'The Jewish people is very dear to me, and I feel – if not every day, then at least every Shabbat – that I am a link in the chain of the generations of the Jewish people. In my opinion,' he continues, 'it is very important that the Jewish people continues to exist in the world and make its spiritual contribution. None the less, I think that I may be permitted to live in the Diaspora, even though I am aware of the sociological statistics indicating that my children will marry non-Jews and will abandon the Jewish people.' My reaction is that such an individual is either a hopeless gambler, or that what he said to begin with – that he holds the Jewish people very close to his heart – is not a very strong feeling. Certainly, far lesser dangers motivate people to try to change their behaviour. When one reads in the newspaper that there is a some danger of contracting certain diseases unless one stops smoking or begins to exercise, many people, particularly in the United States, change their habits, throw away their cigarettes and start jogging around the block every morning. And this is in the case of rather low probability of real danger! But when there is a 50 per cent possibility of mixed marriage, and when you have two children, then it is almost certain that one of them will marry a non-Jew. This awareness does not fit well with the statement that one wants this splendid Jewish people to continue to contribute its gifts to humanity. We must point to this contradiction, to this lack of personal and group responsibility, and we must do so fearlessly.

It is a fact that the challenges to the centrality of Eretz Israel as a place where the majority of the Jewish people should live do not emanate from Israel. This is not some theoretical, neutral, objective idea that may come to one's mind in Jerusalem as well as in New York or Los Angeles or Montevideo. Generally I try to judge things *per se*, and not in terms of the people involved, but one must make note of this phenomenon; the source of the assumption that it is possible to maintain spiritual Jewish centres outside of Israel lies in the Diaspora alone. There is no need to dwell at length on the psychological and the psycho-sociological reasons for this argument.

The problem facing us is no different from the problem that faced the early pioneers of Zionism 100 years ago. The problem is one of a change in the spiritual climate. That is the reason why Zionism was a challenge, and that is the reason why it still is a challenge – particularly for the youth. Israel is, without any doubt, not an easy country in which to be absorbed. It is replete with problems. In the words of the Hebrew poet Tchernichovsky: 'O my country, O my homeland; O mountain of bare rocks'. From the logical point of view, however, it is also possible to reverse the text: 'Mountain of bare rocks, but none the less my homeland'.

Speech to the World Zionist Organization, October 1986

Jerusalem,
Still Under Siege

ABOUT 1920 YEARS AGO, the Romans intended to fortify the northern borders of their empire and therefore, in the year 71 AD, the ninth Roman Legion was ordered to build a fortress which then grew to become the city of Eboracum, which the Vikings later called Yarwik, and which later became York.

At the same time, in the year 70 AD, in a different corner of the Roman empire they planned to destroy a city, so that in the spring of 70 AD four Roman legions – the fifth, the tenth, twelfth, and fifteenth – besieged the city of Jerusalem. They numbered close to 80,000 soldiers compared with only some 25,000 Jews in Jerusalem, the ratio being a little more than 3:1. The siege started on the eve of Pesach of that year; three weeks later the outer wall was penetrated; ten days later the second wall was penetrated; on the ninth of Av the second Temple was set on fire and a month later, on 8 Elul, after five months of siege, the upper city of Jerusalem was set on fire and totally destroyed.

In the same vein, in the second century another Roman emperor, Hadrian, decided again to fortify the borders of the Roman empire at its northern limits, and ordered that a wall be erected along the Tyne Valley. At the same time, that same emperor decided to erase any possible memory of the city of Jerusalem, and decided to call it by his name, Publius Aelius Hadrianus, and to dedicate it to Jupiter Capitolinum. Jerusalem thus became Aelia Capitolina. With a similar aim in mind, in an attempt to erase from human memory the term

52

'Eretz Yisrael', the land of Israel, Hadrian decided to name it 'Syria Palaestina', later known as Palestine.

In the fourth century AD there lived in the town of Bethlehem, near Jerusalem, Hieronimus Sophronius Eusebius, who also became known as St Jerome. He wrote the following observations in his commentary to the book of Zephania:

To this day it is forbidden to the unbelievers [the Jews] to come to Jerusalem. Only for the purpose of mourning are they allowed to come and they must purchase a permit to weep for the destruction of their kingdom – even their tears must be bought. On the anniversary of the destruction of the city by the Romans one could see the unhappy people gather together, old men and old women, the infirm and the weak, all dressed in rags.

Even their tears had to be bought.

Admittedly, in the latter course of the history of our nation, some nations were more generous to us Jews. In years of persecutions, in centuries of pogroms, Jews were allowed to shed tears free of charge, and in 1099, even in the Castle of York.

About 100 years ago, the Zionist movement, headed by Theodore Herzl, decided to put an end to this situation by the establishment of a Jewish state, Hebrew-speaking, in Eretz Yisrael. But that did not come for free, either. And so, 1878 years after the siege by the Roman Legions on Jerusalem, the city came under yet another siege by another legion – this time the Arab Legion of the Hashemites.

The establishment of the State of Israel was declared by David Ben Gurion on Friday 14 May in the afternoon, and the next morning, a Saturday, the Arab Legion crossed the Jordan River at the Damia Bridge, moved towards Jerusalem, conquered the Jewish villages of Neveh Yaacov and Atarot north of Jerusalem, in a concerted effort on the part of five Arab armies (Iraq, Syria, Lebanon, Transjordan and Egypt) to smother the infant-state in its cradle.

The Jewish Quarter in the Old City of Jerusalem came under siege, and after a while, out of 300 soldiers only 36 were left, with only 300 bullets – and therefore they decided to surrender. Jerusalem again fell into the hands of an alien army. The holy places were atrociously desecrated, Jews were barred from praying near the Western Wall. Now they could not even buy their tears. But this time it was not for too long.

In the spring of 1967 Egypt and Syria decided (it sounds strange in this half of the twentieth century, but I'll say it), to annihilate the State of Israel. Despite our warnings, King Hussein 'jackaled-in', attacking Jerusalem in order to share the spoils. Israel responded in accordance with international law, acting in self-defence, and liberated Samaria and Judaea from the Hashemite aggression. And on the 28th of Iyyar, 23 years ago today, Jerusalem was indeed liberated. According to Israeli law, 'The Law, Jurisdiction and Administration of the State shall be applied to any part of Eretz Yisrael as specified in a decree.' Through this legal mechanism Jerusalem became united again, to stay a united city, the capital city of Israel, under Israeli sovereignty forever.

When the Roman emperor Pompeius conquered Eretz Yisrael in 63 BC, he entered the Temple. The Roman historian Tacitus writes the following on this occasion: 'He entered the Temple by the right of his victory', in other words, by the right of his might. But our approach is in full contrast to that of the Romans: the reunification of Jerusalem is a victory of the right of the Jews to their homeland and to their capital city.

Yet for some this is just not good enough. In recent months Jerusalem has again been under siege, this time politically.

The formal approach of the Western democracies, recently led, I regret to say, by the United States, as regards the city of

Jerusalem and its fate, is that the city must remain united. This sounds quite all right, until you hear the rest of it: 'Yes, it should stay united, but the city as a whole must be subject to negotiations in the future.' This would mean even the very site on which our Parliament has rested for so many years should be, according to this position, subject to negotiations some time in the future. Is there any member-state of the United Nations whose sovereignty over its capital city is questioned, 42 years after its establishment? It is not for us to tell Americans if their capital should be Richmond, Virginia, or Washington D.C.; it is not for us to say whether in Britain it should be York or London; but it is only for us to say what will be the fate of our capital city, Jerusalem D.C., David's Capital. It is our prerogative, it is our exclusive right.

And now they tell us that the outskirts of Jerusalem should be designated as occupied territory. They say that our brothers and sisters who are fleeing from threats of new pogroms in the Soviet Union have the right to emigrate from the Soviet Union. But then they also tell us that it is not a good idea to settle in certain parts of their homeland which some people regard as a country belonging to others.

We do insist on the right of any Jew to dwell anywhere in the free world, and of course in any part of our homeland, Eretz Yisrael. They should be able to do so, in the suburb of Gilo, south of Jerusalem, in the suburb of Ramot, north of Jerusalem, in the suburb of Pisgat Ze'ev, east of Jerusalem. But now a question arises: if we do think that it is the right of Jews to live, to settle in Gilo, where actually do we draw the line? If Gilo is all right, maybe the vicinity of Bethlehem should also be considered all right; if Ramot is a place for a Jew to live, where do you draw the line? Is it not true that a few miles north of Jerusalem, north of Ramot, in the cradle of our history, on these hills, Jews have the right to settle?

And sometimes, when I talk with American friends, or

55

diplomats (some of them could be our friends too), or members of Congress, or just good Americans with open ears and mind, I remind them that there is, for instance, a certain town in the US with a very specific history that relates to the Civil War, called Shilo. And I ask them, 'Would you deem it conceivable that the mayor of Shilo in the US would decree that it is illegal for a Jewish family to live in Shilo just because they are Jews, and because some of the Americans over there might be, as they say today, "sensitive" to their living there?' And they say, 'Well, of course, it's inconceivable' therefore I ask, 'Is it conceivable that in the original, biblical Shilo, 20 miles north of Jerusalem, specifically there in their homeland, Jews would be legally barred from dwelling on the basis of their Jewishness? Is this not absurd? Cannot we in this country ask, do Jews have the right to live in London? Do Jews have the right to live in York?' The answer should be a resounding 'yes' – Jews have the right to live everywhere in their homeland, in Eretz Yisrael.

The right of the Jews to their homeland is intimately interwoven with, actually inseparable from, the right of the Jewish State to national security and to self-defence. I think it is very appropriate today to describe the basic difficulties of the State of Israel, *vis-à-vis* its national security, by focusing on European security and on the ongoing talks that started in March about a year ago in Vienna under the acronym CFE, the limitations on the conventional arms in Europe. The significance of these talks, I believe, extends beyond European security, because they afford us an opportunity to define rather rigorously in modern terms what is really a sufficient degree of national security, a very vague notion indeed. But there in Vienna they take the opportunity, and they are trying to define it, at least according to the requirements of the Western democracies of the NATO alliance.

They have come to the conclusion quite a few years ago in

the NATO headquarters, that the core of the security problem of Europe is not the proliferation of nuclear weapons but, on the contrary, the conventional arms and more specifically, the enormous edge in conventional arms between the east and the west, the Warsaw Pact and the NATO allies. The numbers presented last March to the 23 NATO allies by Mr Baker were that the Warsaw Pact can employ some 52,000 tanks while the NATO forces would have to content themselves with only 22,000. The ratio, therefore, is about 2.5:1, considered to be untenable, unacceptable from the point of view of Western national security. They require the ratio to be exactly 1:1; 20,000 on the east, 20,000 on the west. The nice thing about these developments is that under Mr Gorbachev, the Soviets tend, in general terms, and in some respects also in some of the details, to agree with that approach.

Is it not curious that a 1:1 ratio should be the requirement? After all, there has been no war in Europe since the worst of all wars ended 45 years ago. And after all, Western Europe enjoys a strategic depth of at least 300, maybe 400 and even 500 miles across from France, lending them early warning not of a day, not two days, not even six weeks and in the future maybe some months. Is it not the case that today Western Europe faces modern, benevolent regimes working democratically?

With all these details in mind, I think that we should try to project them onto our situation in the Middle East, in order to be able to assess our grim situation in this part of the world. If we focus only on the four Arab countries that compose our Eastern front – Syria, Jordan, Iraq, Saudi Arabia – you will see about 12,000 tanks opposed by fewer than 4000, closer to 3800, on our side. The ratio, therefore, is not 2.5:1, but higher than 3:1. If 2.5:1 is considered unacceptable to Europeans, why should 3:1 be considered acceptable to us? On top of that, compare the distances: a strategic depth not of 200 miles, not even 100; across from the metropolitan area of Tel-Aviv, from the Jordan to the Sea and including 'greater Israel' in the words of some, with Samaria, with Judaea – 45 miles in all.

I do not have to elaborate on the types of regimes that we face, but I think it is still significant to mention that in the first experiment in democracy which any country other than Israel has undergone lately, the result in the Hashemite Kingdom of Jordan is that 40 per cent of the Jordanian Parliament are by now fundamentalist Muslims. And then we have Iraq, and we have Lebanon, and we have Beirut, and maybe as a token of the type of political atmosphere that we have to face in our part of the world, let us mention that recently not only Muslims fight Christians, not only Druze fight Muslims, but two Christian factions – one Samir Jaja's, the other Michel Aoun's – are going for each other's jugulars, as well as two Shiite factions: the Amal and the Hizb'Allah.

To borrow a term from my past geological exerience, I think we can say that we actually live on the margin, and sometimes on the top, of a political and military volcano in our part of the Middle East. When Europeans come for a visit, we sometimes have discussions, and we tell them that we are not spoiled, we are not pampered, we do not look for any special treatment. But we ask for fairness, and we ask that Europeans apply to us the same standards of national security that they would like to be applied to their own children. We also have some children to raise in our part of the world.

In recent months, in the last two years or so, violence has been taking place in Samaria, in Judaea, in the Gaza district, with some spill-over into Israel proper within its pre-1967 borderlines. The far-reaching goal of this violence has been defined again and again during these years by the then Defence Minister of our country, Mr Yitzchak Rabin, well esteemed by many of us, a distinguished commander of our

58

army, Chief of Staff during the 1967 Six-Day War. He has time and again defined their goal as ousting Israel from Judaea, Samaria, the Gaza district and East Jerusalem 'as a minimum', I repeat as a *minimum*. This is in full conformity with some statements made by some Arab leaders. I will quote one, the Butcher of Baghdad, Saddam Hussein:

Thirty kilometres are enough in order to break the back of Israel. A number of kilometres are enough so that Israel will collapse. – The Camp David agreements are rejected; we are ready to accept a solution that will restore to the Arabs and to Iraq full rights in Palestine without shedding blood. The solution is that Palestine will be returned to the Arabs and the Arabs will return to Palestine – all of Palestine.

This is in accordance with a document that I received here last year, printed by an organization called PSC, Palestine Solidarity Campaign:

Palestine Solidarity Campaign (PSC) was founded in 1982 to promote support in Britain for the Palestinian people ...

Aims: – to support the Palestinian people's inalienable right to establish an independent state in any part of Palestine freed from Zionist rule, towards forming a secular, democratic state in the whole of Palestine.

These words, taken together, summed together across the board, coming from all different Arab sources, should be taken seriously; I do believe and I so propose, and I have been in science for quite some time. Yesterday I visited with some of my colleagues in the University of Leeds, in the Geology Department, and in the Geography Department, and we talked science, threw some graphs on the board. It was really a pleasant day, and it reminds me that with the number of publications that I have had the opportunity to publish, even in a distinguished British journal, I think I know all the tricks of how to qualify one's statements. Some that come to my mind would be: 'It is possible that'; 'it seems that'; 'it is

59

reasonable to suggest'; 'it can safely be assumed'; 'there is some likelihood that'; 'it cannot be altogether precluded that' – and more.

You can invent the rest of them, but I have no hesitation whatsoever in saying that in Samaria, in Judaea, and in the Gaza district, the situation has developed into an either/or situation, or to use computer language, a zero-one situation. In binary language, either Israel controls the whole area west of the Jordan River, or the PLO terrorist organization takes over. Another version: either Israel controls the whole area west of the Jordan River, or the fundamentalist Islamic terrorist movement of the Hamas takes over. Another version: either Israel controls the whole area or a certain mix of the two takes over.

In the last year or so, about 200 Arabs were atrociously killed by other Arabs, signalling to us that relinquishing the areas Samaria, Judaea and the Gaza district will bring about only one possible result: the Lebanonization, or the Beirutization of these areas. And I shall render that the PLO or any of the other terrorist groups must not be allowed to establish yet another terrorist state between Syria, Iraq and Libya, when we all know that the next step is going to be the spill-over towards the Galilee, some signs of which we have already seen.

The situation is indeed quite complex, the dangers are numerous and therefore it should be understood by all those who are objective, who have open ears and open minds, why so many Israelis, when they have to choose, would rather be harshly criticized than eloquently eulogized.

This visit of my dear wife and myself has been part of an official visit of ours at the invitation of Her Majesty's Government. It is very generous indeed, and they have put together a very nice programme, with important and interesting meetings, with some sightseeing too. Last week we had the opportunity to sit in the Strangers' Gallery in the House of Commons, during Prime Minister's Question Time. The day before, I had the opportunity to spend twenty minutes in Westminster Abbey, where I saw, among others in this immense, amazing conservation of English history, the statues of Peel, of Gladstone, and Disraeli – standing near each other, but of course not facing each other. And when I sat in the Strangers' Gallery, looking at the green seats of the chambers, I could almost see them shutting up Disraeli about 100 years ago; I could almost hear him saying, 'One day I will speak and you will hear me.' I could almost hear Churchill denouncing his government for selling Czechoslovakia down the river for an illusion of a European stability, telling them, 'You chose dishonour and you will have war.'

I anticipated fireworks between the Prime Minister and Mr Kinnock, but there were almost none. The reason was, quite appropriately, that it was after the IRA's exploding a bomb where a soldier, married with two children, lost his life. Mr Kinnock then chose to declare, rather than ask, that it be the unanimous policy of the House of Commons not to surrender to violence, and this statement met with the traditional British 'hear-hear'. Let me concur with this policy – we must not surrender to violence.

We have proposed the Camp David framework as a policy. It entails a gradual approach, a transitional period, an interim agreement; a decrease in friction through Arab autonomy; the seeking of a peace treaty with Jordan, and open-ended negotiations on the complex issue of contradicting claims to sovereignty in Samaria, Judaea and Gaza.

Although the idea was rejected by the European countries in the Venice declaration ten years ago, we must hope that it will be understood, that this is the single plausible path to pursue on the road to understanding and peaceful coexistence in our troubled part of the world.

61

At the end of the Haftara chapter of this week's Torah portion, Jeremiah 32, we read a story from the days of the ancient siege on Jerusalem, by Nebuchadnazzar, King of Babylon 2600 years ago, in which Jeremiah consoles the Jewish people:

Fields will be bought, and deeds will be signed, sealed and witnessed in the region of Binyamin, and in the outskirts of Jerusalem, and in the towns of Judaea and in the towns of the hill-country and in the towns of the foothills and in the towns of the Negev, as I will gather them again, said the Lord.

Speech in London, 22 May 1990, celebrating the liberation and unification of Jerusalem in 1967

Back to the High Road

THE LAST election campaign was essentially a referendum. The Labour Party presented a clear proposal to the national agenda: the relinquishing of parts of Eretz Yisrael to foreign rule, through the pressure-mechanism of an international conference. Yet even with the support of Israel's Arab citizens, the Labour Party was unable to convince the majority of this view, which was rejected by the voter. And so, this item was removed from the agenda, and last week Labour leaders themselves sealed the decision of the voter with their promise that the concept of an international conference would not be included in the basic guidelines of the government which they attempted to establish. For the sake of peace they were prepared, in their words, 'to wear a shtreimel'; but it appears that for the right to wear a shtreimel they are prepared to abandon the single means, in their eyes, to bring peace to our region.

A great challenge stands before us in the diplomatic arena: the return of Israel's foreign policy back to the high road, after having been led down dead-end alleys for the past two years. The Arabs jumped at the idea of an international conference (originally conceived in the Kremlin in 1981), not as a means for achieving peace. In their eyes, such a conference is a safe diplomatic plot to push Israel back to its 1967 borders, while avoiding Israel's demand for *direct negotiations with no prior conditions*. It is a fact: in George Shultz's letter of 4 March 1988, the vital term 'direct negotiations' was not mentioned at all. In its place we find the odd sentence: 'The parties to each bilateral negotiation will determine the procedure and agenda of their negotiation'.

63

The innocent listener will ask: 'Why not simply agree to direct negotiations?' And the reply, of course, is that 'to this the Arabs would refuse'. The listener then continues to ask: 'Does not such a refusal signify that they are still not ready to tell their people: "Here are the Jews whom we love to hate: we have decided to change our basic position and directly negotiate with them, in order to sign a peace treaty"?'

The peace treaty, as the practical goal of direct negotiations between two warring sides, has also disappeared down the dark alleys where Israeli diplomacy has been dragged over the past two years. According to the decade-old document entitled 'Framework for Peace in the Middle East', as agreed upon at Camp David, 'the parties are determined to reach a just, comprehensive, and durable settlement of the Middle East conflict through the conclusion of peace treaties ...'. However, the peace accord is not mentioned in the declaration of the European Market countries in Venice (23 June 1980), nor in the Hussein–Peres agreement in London (11 April 1987). The authors of all these are content with the hazy term 'comprehensive peace', or its blurry surrogate 'peaceful settlement', but even the cease-fire treaties signed between us and our neighbours in 1949 were actually 'peaceful settlements'. Thus we have allowed the Arabs to lead us down a side alley, like a woman with whom one does not walk on the lighted boulevard. Thus we allow them to appear before the world as seekers of peace, while they continue to poison their people with hatred for the Jews and their single country.

When we speak of direct negotiations with no prior conditions, our intent is that no party place conditions on their participation in talks. Each side can bring its position to the negotiations, even if it is far from the other party's views. But do not ask us to relinquish our position as a condition to sit with us at the negotiating table.

'Ahh', the hasty critic will react to these words, 'Polemics', 'hollow slogans', 'legalisms'. There is nothing to fear from such criticism. All of the US Secretary of State's efforts the past two years were aimed at reaching a verbal alchemist's formula to draw the Hashemite king from the throes of Arab brotherhood. Hussein's speech on 31 July 1988 proved that such a text has not been found. He has remained in the shell and we remain with the burnt stew.

We must, then, return to the one formula that can be presented, simply and effectively, with a defendable internal logic. We will demand *direct negotiations, with no prior conditions*, with our neighbouring states for a single purpose: signing peace accords between us. Each party will come with his position – we will come with our position as detailed in the Camp David accords.

The rehabilitation of Israel's foreign policy demands a period of stability, whose condition is a government resting on a solid majority in the Knesset. This leads to the conclusion
that it is necessary to invest an effort in including the Labour Party in the Israeli government headed by Yitzchak Shamir. An outside viewer may claim that there is an inconsistency in this article, between its opening polemics and its conciliatory conclusion. Yet in our complex reality we compromise between many contradictions, by an ongoing attempt to separate the important from the trivial. This is not always simple, but the effort is always worthwhile.

Israel's political high road is clearly marked, both in procedure and essence. Only steadfast and consistent travel on this path will eventually bring us to the positive goal to which we all aspire.

Ha'aretz, 18 November 1988

The Only Game in Town

AN ATTEMPT TO apply Western diplomacy to the Middle East must take into account that the Middle East political scene is different. It is characterized by shifting alliances and broken agreements; by authoritarian military regimes, manipulation of the media, political violence and, in some instances by State-sponsored, brutal, international terrorism. Recent events demonstrate that the Middle East has become a laboratory for an incredible transplant of seventh-century fanaticism into the twentieth century, by the reactionary Shiite Revolution.

The State of Israel has stood for four decades in the zone of collision between the Western World and this Mid-Eastern political underworld. Israel has weathered periodic attempts to eradicate it, and has withstood incessant terrorist atrocities. In contrast to other Western countries that became involved in conflicts, Israel cannot afford to order its soldiers back to their ships and 'Home by Christmas'. It continues to face a formidable threat: With a width of only 50 miles, Israel faces on its eastern front alone Syria, Jordan, Saudi Arabia and Iraq – about 1,200,000 men and 10,600 tanks!

Are tanks and topography relevant to modern warfare? The US Secretary of Defense, Frank C. Carluci, recently called upon the Soviets to eliminate 'The Warsaw Pact's numerical superiority over NATO in tanks, artillery and other offensive arms', since these 'could be used to invade, seize and hold territory in Western Europe'. Yet Israel is encouraged to swallow the fallacious argument that the Gaza District, Samaria and Judaea do not count in the missile era. Faced with tank forces about half that of NATO's forces in Europe, Israel, by relinquishing these areas, will put its head in a noose.

Some people, while acknowledging that the Land of Israel belongs as of right to the Jewish Nation, support the concept of a 'territorial compromise'. After 20 years they should realize that King Hussein's reaction to it ('totally unacceptable') is not just an opening posture. From his point of view, the main theme of the concept is not what he is apt to gain, but rather what he is supposed to give up. For a Hashemite King to agree to transfer even the smallest of a sacred Arab land to a Jewish state is an impossibility.

It has been shown recently that even if the Hashemites wanted to they would not be able to control the so-called 'West Bank'. If they try, the combination of internal dissension and external Arab diplomatic and military pressure will force them out within weeks. Therefore, if Israel relinquishes even parts of Judaea or Samaria to the Jordanians, the inevitable outcome will be the establishment of a PLO State. To agree to the creation of yet another pro-Soviet, terrorist State between Syria and Libya, by default or by proxy, is folly for Israel, the United States and the Free World. Many Israelis understand, therefore, that some paths recently advocated for Israelis will expose them to threats that are far more dangerous than the difficulties these proposals claim to alleviate.

We have been told in recent months that Secretary of State Shultz's 'Peace Plan', which is the basis for his current Middle East diplomacy, is 'the only game in town'. That may be true for Washington, but the real game is played in the Middle East itself, and it is much simpler. It entails only two principles: (a) they want to destroy us, and (b) we insist on keeping alive. The game is simple because a gun-barrel, as well as a clear document such as the PLO charter, are self-explanatory.

A modest but realistic diplomatic goal for a Middle East diplomacy should now aim at retaining relative stability. Misconceptions in the minds of Arab leaders concerning an imminent rift between the United States and Israel may obviously destabilize the region. Adherence to the Camp David Accords, which have no significance in the Shultz document, as well as total dedication to the concept of direct negotiations – a term which was substituted by the stillborn hybrid of bilateral negotiations within an international parley – are examples of constructive statements. Only after the Arabs realize that Israel is here to stay will the day come when peace will be made possible in that corner of the world. The continuing alliance between the United States and a strong Israel will hasten its arrival.

Jerusalem, Early Thursday Morning

JERUSALEM, 4:00 A.M. early Thursday morning. Rain. I have just returned from a direct broadcast to an American television station, where I was asked to respond to the American government's announcement that it is opening a dialogue with the organization which works to free Palestine from its Jewish presence. These media people are fast; they received the news, couldn't find anyone else at home, went over the list, and found me at the bottom. A phone call at 2:30, a hurried entrance to the studio, two minutes before the broadcast I'm hooked up to a microphone, my red tie straightened. 'Atlanta, do you hear us?' 'Yes' 'What do you have to say about this new situation?' I answered as best I could. MK Ran Cohen, in a dark suit and blue tie, is at my side. Like myself, he certainly wants things to go well. His opinion is different. It's a pity.

We must deal with the real argument. The apparent disagreement is whether this version or another by Arafat is ample expression of PLO moderation, but this is not the real topic on the agenda. The basic argument is whether the State of Israel should or can allow the establishment of an Arab state west of the Jordan. A comparative analysis of the PLO's statements is only marginal to the argument, even though it is what fills the newspapers and the air and the television screens.

I dare say that most of the people who support the

69

establishment of a PLO state are not actually interested in the question of whether the PLO has changed its traditional purpose – wiping the State of Israel off the map. Advising Israel to agree to a PLO state exempts these people from having to make calculations about the proposed plans of this country's leaders. The real conclusions are totally different: the basic premise is that Israel must return to its 1967 borders and hand over Samaria, Judaea, and the Gaza district to foreign rule. There are those who originally thought this foreign power would be Hashemite State of Jordan, but, they claim with a shrug of their shoulders, if Hussein does not want it, or cannot handle it, Arafat and cohorts will rule: what can we do, just as long as Israel gets out of those areas?

This assertion can be proven by checking the diplomatic time table. It is common knowledge that in 1977 the PLO did not fulfil the conditions set by the US in 1975, as a test of its moderation. Nevertheless, in March 1977 President Jimmy Carter demanded that Israeli Prime Minister Yitzchak Rabin agree to PLO participation in the Geneva Convention. It was common knowledge that the PLO did not change its statements in 1980. Nevertheless, in 1980 representatives of the European Market proclaimed in Venice that Israel must agree to realize the right of self-determination of the Arabs of Judaea, Samaria and the Gaza district, and to the participation of the PLO as their representative in the negotiations. It is clear that Arafat did not change anything in his speech before the European Parliament in Strasbourg last summer, and nevertheless French Foreign Minister Rolan Duma rushed from Paris to shake the hand of the man who was denied a visa to enter the US because he is a killer. And in Israel? For years local public figures have advocated a unilateral Israeli withdrawal, first from the Gaza strip in the opinion of some, or simultaneously from Samaria and Judaea, according to others. One result of such a secession would be handing over the

the area to the PLO, but these recommendations were made long before PLO leaders agreed to alter their standard text.

If so, why the excessive preoccupation with PLO statements? The answer is clear: Those who have decided long ago that Israel must retreat to the 1949 cease-fire lines in any case, understand that it is difficult to sell such an idea to the great majority of the Israeli public. In order to promote this plan, they must wrap it attractively in a slogan which calms the intellect, a formula which numbs the senses.

So what, they say, give the PLO a chance. Examine them through negotiations. According to this logic of an examination, we are only at the beginning of the slippery slope. They can tell us again and again, 'Try it, Arafat is promising, take a chance. You allow them to set up a PLO state and we will give you security assurances.' In other words, roulette: 'Close your eyes, throw the dice, take a step, and afterwards – you'll see, it'll be all right.' It will not be all right! There are two stages in the PLO plan and we must not fall victim to political deceit, 15 years after having fallen victim to military deceit.

Our Zionist stand rests on two pillars: the right of the Jewish people to Eretz Yisrael and the right of the Jewish State to national security. In order to fulfil the latter, we must practically implement the former in all of western Eretz Yisrael.

In the coming months no one will speak with us about the 'General's Plan', about 'territorial compromise', or about Israeli sovereignty over the Jordan valley. They will talk instead about abandoning the areas to PLO murderers and about realizing Stage A of their plan.

It is already morning in Jerusalem, and it is still rainy. I would like to conclude these thoughts with the same words that have closed my speeches these past few months and that can serve as the basis for broad national consensus these days,

71

in the light of the danger confronting us, it is our country and we shall defend it!

Ha'aretz, 16 December 1988

The Camp David
Formula Awaits
Rediscovery

IT IS SUITABLE to open a current political discussion on the troubled Middle East with a reference to the literary world. The sentencing to death of Salman Rushdie by Islamic fundamentalists is a reminder that Israel has always been fighting for survival in the actual zone of collision between Western civilization and a violent Islamic political subculture. The amazing experiment in transplanting the seventh-Century concept of jihad, or holy war, to the twentieth century was tried on the Jewish state of 'non-believers' while it was still in its cradle.

This incessant attempt to annihilate Israel has found new ways, now aiming at the establishment of a PLO terrorist state in Judea, Samaria and the Gaza district. It would, no doubt, serve as a launching pad for expansion: first eastward, eliminating King Hussein, and then westward, liquidating Israel, with the backing of more than 11,000 tanks and 1.9 million soldiers stationed in the four Arab countries east of the Jordan River. No Israeli or American in his right mind should agree to the establishment of another version of Libya only 50 miles south of Syria, either directly or by proxy or by default. And since Israelis understand the nature of this threat, most of them would rather be unjustly criticized than be poetically eulogized.

Regrettably, the surge in US diplomatic activism has not positively contributed to the cause of peace in the Middle East. Starting with the American tendency to consider the Soviet-born concept of an international tribunal on the Middle East, it continued in the Shultz document of 4 March 1988 which voided the essential transitional period embodied in the Camp David accords. This suggested that the United States is considering divorcing itself from the accords. It culminated in the US initiation of dialogue with the PLO murderers, legitimizing both the Arab violence directed against Jews in the land of Israel and the PLO terrorist raids across the Israel–Lebanon border. All in all, by yielding to Arab pressure, the United States signalled to the Arab juhadists that time is on their side, thus rendering the situation far less ripe for solution than it could be. The Soviet foreign minister's recent embrace of both Syria and the PLO, and his harsh words about sanctions against Israel, proved again that anything you can do he can do better.

In view of these dire straits, the creativity of the Camp David compromise, as initiated by Israel a decade ago, is outstanding. As too many people reject it outright, it may be helpful here to give a quick sketch of the framework for peace in the Middle East as agreed to by the United States, Israel and Egypt:

- Israel will be responsible for its security in the whole area west of the Jordan River
- The Arab inhabitants of Samaria, Judea and Gaza will enjoy autonomy through a freely elected self-governing authority
- As a substantial confidence-building measure, that authority will be in effect for a transitional period of five years. Within this period, the final status of Judea, Samaria and the Gaza district will be negotiated. The

74

agreement on the final status will be an integral part of the comprehensive peace treaty between Israel and the Hashemite Kingdom of Jordan.

We have a clear position concerning Judea, Samaria and the Gaza district: they are part of Eretz Yisrael, the Land of Israel which belongs by right to the Jewish people; we must keep it, we intend to keep it and we shall keep it. However, we are aware that others have their own claims for the same areas.

In this context, the Camp David compromise offers the transitional period as a mechanism to defer resolution of the complex issue of sovereignty, with the hope that building mutual confidence will render the situation more manageable and the problems riper for solution. It is important to note that the framework is open-ended. There is nothing in the accord itself that precludes any agreed solution for the final status of the disputed areas.

It has become fashionable to label the Camp David achievement as junk. Not only is this shortsighted, it also indicates a short memory. It may surprise some that as late as January 1988, in an interview with the Kuwaiti newspaper *Al-Anaba*, the Egyptian President, Hosni Mubarak, offered the following pertinent observations:

Camp David includes two documents, one for the solution of the Egyptian-Israeli problem and the other, which is the general framework of principles according to which the Palestinian problem is to be solved in all its aspects. That is, this is not a binding agreement but a method for a solution on which we shall agree through general points. The first document ended in the Egyptian–Israeli treaty and the return of the Sinai to Egypt. As for the second document, concerning the resolution of the Palestinian problem in all its aspects, when we discussed it with the Israelis, I realized that our brothers attacked Egypt because she tried to reach a solution of the Palestinian problem. Had we continued the talks on the second framework of Camp David, we would have been in a better situation, in stages.

Yes, indeed. In the last decade, no substantially new ideas were offered to alleviate the difficulties in our corner of the Middle East. The Camp David compromise still rises high above any of the non-starter formulas, being practical, gradual, generous and wise. It should be given a fresh look and a new chance.

The Eighth Option

DESPAIR. That's the conclusion that must be reached, based on the study of the Jaffee Center for Strategic Studies in Tel Aviv University, 'Judaea, Samaria, and Gaza: Options for Peace', and its companion, 'Israel and the Territories – Towards a Solution'.

The authors detail six alternative solutions to the present situation in western Eretz Israel, rejecting them all. In their opinion, those options which would ensure secure borders to Israel are not acceptable to the Arabs, while those acceptable to the Arabs contradict all necessary security requirements for Israel. In short, they conclude, it is a dead end. The authors offer a seventh alternative for a solution: the establishment of a Palestinian state following a 15-year autonomy. Yet, while compiling their proposal, a funny thing happened to the authors: they abandoned the rigorous standards of analysis that they applied to the other proposals, and raised an option that is amazingly detached from Middle East reality.

In order to prove this claim, one has only to read the report and quote it:

Israel's vulnerability and consequent security requirements dictate that the Palestinian entity that would evolve in the course of the process be a highly constrained one, for which there are few precedents in modern history.

The authors provide an example of such a constraint in their requirement that there 'must be Israeli control of the airspace above the West Bank and Gaza, both for air force training flights (a problem that has no solution within the boundaries of "little" Israel) and for early warning and intelligence flights'.

What is the chance of actually reaching an agreement which would include conditions the authors have termed 'minimal security arrangements'? They even suggest we sign this agreement with the PLO, and on top of that, 'any attempt to reach a settlement must provide for adequate dissuasion of Syria or, alternatively – if at all possible – its constructive involvement in a solution that deals with its own conflict with Israel'. Yet the authors are not satisfied with this severe demand on Middle East reality; they add that 'the settlement must be ratified by the surrounding Arab world through the vehicle of peace treaties with Israel'.

An expression of a similarly detached approach to Middle East reality, and to the disregard by the fanatic Islam world of signed agreements with 'non-believers', is found in their additional suggestions:

An additional provision designed to diminish the danger of a future Israeli-Palestinian conflict should comprise constitutional prohibitions in both states against irredentist activity. Moreover, the two states should undertake to honour their contractual commitments to one another even in the event of regime or constitutional changes in one or both of them, or in Jordan.

That is, an Israel totally stripped of its security assets, will rely on the commitments of PLO-Arafat that when PLO-Abu Musa takes control of the State of Palestine, or when the fundamentalist Islamic 'Hamas' defeats them both, they will honour their contracted obligations. It is hard to believe these words have been written in Hebrew, in Tel Aviv, just a few hours' drive from Amman, Damascus, and Beirut.

However, the hardest blow to the seventh, baseless alternative is dealt to it by the Jaffee Center report itself, beginning on page 166, in their summary analysis of the imminent dangers in relinquishing Judaea and Samaria to foreigners, creating a situation in which the Arabs are tempted to 'violate the demilitarization agreements, and later – if appropriate countermeasures were not taken – an attack fraught with danger for Israel'; that is, let us clarify, at a distance of 15 kilometres from Natanya. The report's authors add important arguments to prove the dangers to Israel's existence in abandoning parts of Eretz Yisrael, even to those who are willing to sign a piece of paper with us. It is clear that there is no chance to sign an agreement, even under the minimal security conditions as defined by the Jaffee Center staff, with those factors whom the authors insist on including in the agreement: the PLO and Syria. In any case, the Center's own strategic analysis points out that even if we have an agreement, we would not have peace.

Therefore, if this is the best result of the Center's creativity, the dangerous conclusion may be despair and an abandonment of the peace process. We must then return to the drawing board and come up with the outline of a programme intended to advance us towards a peace based on Israel's security needs, which include the following:

1. Israel will be responsible for its own security west of the Jordan River.
2. In order to minimize friction with the Arab inhabitants of Samaria, Judaea, and the Gaza district, a mechanism that would enable them to manage their day-to-day life should be defined. Such a mechanism is the Administrative Council, to be freely elected by intimidation.
3. A transitional period of a few years is needed as a confidence-building measure between the Arabs of Samaria, Judaea, and Gaza, and the Jewish citizens of Israel, before reaching a settlement on the final status of these areas.

79

4. The agreement between Israel and the Arabs of these areas on the structure, the powers and the responsibilities of the Administrative Council cannot stand alone; its scope must be enlarged towards a more comprehensive peace accord between Israel and the Hashemite Kingdom of Jordan.
5. The issue of sovereignty in the disputed areas is complicated and sensitive. Therefore, in order to advance the process and permit the opening of negotiations, an agreement that would defer the definition of the final status of these areas is needed. It is preferable that the agreement, which will serve as the basis for the negotiations, will not include anything that excludes any solution of the final status. Of course, our own position must be clear, first and foremost to ourselves, yet the agreement on the initial talks must be open-ended towards the future.

These five components are both necessary and sufficient for the initiation of negotiations. He who rejects them and demands creative new ideas of Israel, is not referring to just any ideas but to those which they know in advance will be accepted by the Arabs. Under today's political conditions, while the European position is clear and the US is conducting an open dialogue with the PLO, and while our leftists offer us 'Peace Now' without answering the question, 'And what then?', it is clear that it alludes to the new idea of our agreement to establishing a PLO state, a realization of Stage 1 in its two-stage plan.

These components are logical, reasonable, practical and even generous. They constitute a complete plan under the title 'Framework for Peace in the Middle East as Agreed at Camp David'. True, the Jaffee Center report rejects the Camp David Accords and suggests an alternative which is characterized by two elements: it endangers Israel but it will not be accepted by those whose agreement, according to the authors, is crucial. And if the Arabs again reject our proposal, what then? The logical conclusion, actually arising from the study itself, is simple and forms the basis for further national consensus: standing firm.

Ma'ariv, 14 April 1989

Light at the End of the Cloud

I CAME TO this House on the basis of a Zionist stand which is founded on two moral pillars: the right of the Jewish people to Eretz Yisrael, and the right of the Jewish State to national security. These two rights are inseparable, because national security for Israel cannot be achieved without Israeli control over the entire area west of the Jordan River.

The logical, immediate political ramifications are twofold: 1, there will not be foreign sovereignty in Western Eretz Yisrael; and 2, the State of Israel, and only the State of Israel, shall be responsible for its security in Western Eretz Yisrael. These are the foundations that define the political manoeuvring space of the State of Israel. Within this space, and only within it, we should – and can – strive for peace with our neighbouring countries, search for a peaceful co-existence with the Arabs of Eretz Yisrael, and, in the absence of a partner for talks, create the international political conditions that will allow Israel to maintain its power.

I assume that not everyone in this House agrees with the basic Zionist tenets as I have defined them. But I believe that these conclusions can and should be common to many of us, certainly to many in the Labour Party. It is clear to anyone with eyes in his head, especially in the past year, that a situation has been created where, regardless of many high hopes and many political theories, it is an either–or situation: either we control the area or the PLO does. There is no possibility, even for those who believed there was, of realizing the concept of territorial compromise. There can never be, as there has never been, an agreement with the Hashemite dynasty on the basis of relinquishing parts of our homeland to that dynasty, and there is no need to elaborate in this House on the ramifications of establishing a PLO state. I will, however, mention the words of this year's Israel Prize winner and spokesman, Yaacov Hazan, a year and a half ago that 'a Palestinian state would be a time-bomb for the State of Israel'.

The violence in Samaria, Judaea, and the Gaza district understandably attracts public attention these days. But let us not forget the source of the real threat to Israel's existence, which stems from the eastern front: more than 11,000 tanks, two million soldiers of whom one million are in the standing armies, 13,000 APCs, 1600 fighter planes, over 7000 artillery pieces, and the recent addition of long-range yet accurate ballistic missiles.

We sometimes tend to forget, but we must remind ourselves once in a while that we live under extremely difficult conditions, in a violent, totalitarian, volatile environment. It cannot be merely a coincidence that among the 21 Arab states which have been free from the yoke of colonialism for at least one or two generations, none has succeeded in establishing a democracy. Political violence, it must be concluded, in this era, and I say this regretfully, is inherent in the Arab society, maybe even in Islam, and in this generation it is directed towards the Jewish State.

The conflict between us and the Arab Nation has deep historical and psychological roots. What is Hebron to us, they call El-Halil; Ashkelon for us is Majdal to them; our Shechem is their Nablus; Jerusalem to us is Urshulim-El-Kuds. Such a conflict cannot be ended by a quick fix. When members of this House demand 'Peace now', it is our responsibility as members of the Knesset to ask them, 'And what then?'

This situation dictates a careful approach; the need for caution demands a gradual approach. And this need for gradation leads to the idea of an interim period of a few years before establishing the final status of Samaria, Judaea, and the Gaza district, a period which should be utilized to build trust on both sides between ourselves and the Arabs of Eretz Yisrael.

This is, of course, the basis for the Camp David Accord, which was ratified in the Knesset 11 years ago. Those who were Members of the Knesset in those days will certainly remember that along with the blessings, the Accords were also received with laments, warnings and dark prophecies. In reality, after 11 years, we see dozens of Jewish settlements flowering, breathing, expanding in the Gaza district, in Judaea and in Samaria, even in the past year and a half, with all the violence, all the rocks, all the Molotov cocktails, just as was promised twelve years ago today, on 17 May 1977, that there would be 'many more Elone More's'. There are many more Elone More's.

I turn to Members of the Knesset from all factions: if you desire to know the source of the spirit and strength of our pioneers, go to the Jewish settlements in Samaria, in Judaea and in the Gaza district. Visit there; do not speak to the men – speak to the mothers, see how they live. See how they hold up, how they send their children each morning, even small children, to kindergarten and to school, with all the violence, the rocks, the explosive cocktails, the attempted murders – they stand, live and grow. It is an honour to us all.

I turn again to the members of the Labour Party: I take your platform seriously, and on that basis I can inform the Jewish residents living in Samaria, Judaea and the Gaza district that, realistically, they have already achieved the status of national consensus because, according to the Labour Party platform of the past elections, under the conditions of any diplomatic agreement, Jewish settlements will not be dismantled.

The government's initiative which the Prime Minister presented to the House is based, of course, on the Framework for Peace in the Middle East, as agreed upon at Camp David. It is an important, positive and useful initiative, a framework whose details we have not yet been asked to fill in. There is no need to enumerate the imminent dangers, as they are known to us all, not just to those who oppose it. We must certainly stand on our guard.

Nevertheless, in this context I would like to say that it is of course impossible to have diplomatic progress in an atmosphere of violence. The Arab violence must cease, in accordance with the guidelines of this government, as shared by all it components.

Secondly, it is clear that members of the illegal murderous terrorist groups of the PLO cannot participate in the process. I support the Defence Minister's view that the place for those who inform us that they are members of the PLO, or who we know are members of the PLO, is only in jail.

I would like to add – since the issue was raised and because different interpretations were suggested to the fact that this plan is based on the Camp David Accords – that the establishment of yet another Arab state is not a legitimate right of the Arabs of Eretz Yisrael, especially as we know that such a state would be eventually established on the ruins of the State of Israel.

Our American friends could play an important role in the political process, which may begin or be renewed as a result of the present government's initiative, presented here for approval this evening. They could, but it is not at all clear that they are actually capable of accepting such a role. We must say to them that they must first clarify to themselves and finally understand just how narrow Israel's manoeuvring space is, and what are its political red lines. If they understand this they should, and I hope they can and will want to, make it clear to the Arabs that violence will not chase us away, violence will not move us from that stand which the Prime Minister has presented before the Knesset today.

We must also tell them that, as opposed to what is occasionally said, the violence in Samaria, in Judaea and in the Gaza district, is fuelled not by despair but by its opposite – hope. In these past few months, especially in the wake of the opening of the shameful dialogue between the US Ambassador Peletro and PLO representatives in Tunis, the American stand has been a source of hope for the Arabs of Eretz Yisrael who have adopted violence.

There are members of this Knesset who oppose the government's initiative, and speak of the need to stand strong. I would like to tell these members that it is not enough to speak of resolve; it is necessary to create the appropriate tools for such a national position. In these times, one of the most important tools for establishing our national resolve is national unity, which is expressed in this government's composition. Any attempt to weaken its structure and its stability will only undermine our ability to stand firm, as they themselves demand. I therefore call on these members who still waver, who have notified us that they may abstain or not participate in the vote, to come and vote and support the government initiative which has been put forth by the Prime Minister.

We neither deny nor disregard the fact that these days our skies are clouded. In a poem expressing her longing for better days, the poet Leah Goldberg wrote: 'And you'll go in the field that is wet, and the calm will broaden within you – as the light at the end of the cloud'. If we act on the basis of the unity of goals, the unity of actions and the unity of hearts – as the prophet Isaiah has said: 'Each shall assist his friend and shall tell his brother be strong' – if we act in this manner then the cloud will be overcome by the light.

Speech before the Knesset, 17 May 1989

US Clarifications to the PLO

THERE ARE TWO main schools of thought in this House and in the public pertaining to the problem of Jews and Arabs in Eretz Yisrael. One bases itself on the assumption that there is a moral and practical need to end Israeli rule in Samaria, Judaea and the Gaza district. Two solutions ensue in this case. One is Israeli withdrawal more or less to the 1967 borders, and the relinquishing of these areas. The second solution, emanating from that same basis, suggests disengagement from the Arabs in Samaria, Judaea and the Gaza district by deporting them.

The second school of thought, followed by the Likud and others, rests on the assumption that there is an inseparable combination of the right of the Jewish people to Eretz Yisrael and the right of the Jewish State to national security.

Our approach leads to the recognition that it is possible to achieve co-existence with respect, though not love, between Jews and Arabs: all Jews, including those who have yet to arrive, and all Arabs west of the Jordan River. We assume that this is based, beyond the troubles, beyond the violence, on basic interests common to both Jews and Arabs. This recognition leads to hope, which is also the hope that lies at the base of the government's peace initiative of 14 May 1989, the hope that the Arab side too will understand that these mutual interests exist, and that this can lead to an agreement based on Camp David principles, at least for an interim period.

This hope, that there will be an agreement and soon if possible, absorbed many blows last year, especially by our friends and allies in the United States. It was a year ago that Secretary of State George Schultz announced that the US held what he termed 'substantive dialogue' with the PLO through Ambassador Peletro in Tunis. The second blow came last week, with the publishing of five clarifications by the US to the PLO.

Of these five I would like to bring two before you. The first: 'The US will not establish the PLO's role in the process, the PLO will, by its actions and deeds'. The second: 'The US recognizes the reality that the Palestinian Arabs will not participate in the process without permission from the PLO, and the US knows that the Palestinians await this permission'.

In other words, the unavoidable conclusion is that the US is announcing that it affords the PLO an important, even central role in the diplomatic process. This American administration position, which has not been denied since its publication, stands of course in clear contrast to the basic guidelines of the Israeli government, with the government decision of 4 May 1989, and certainly with the Cabinet decision of 5 November 1989.

We should perhaps ask ourselves why, when the US government, its advisers, clerks and officials, are aware of Israel's stand, do they see fit to adopt such a stand, even making it publicly known? These are not evil people, these are really our friends, and they certainly want what is good for us.

But what explanation, or one of the explanations, or a partial explanation, can I offer? There is a school of thought in the American administration, possibly the ruling one, that it is process-oriented, which aims at the process and is not end-product-oriented, which pays more attention to the process and less to the possible outcome of a political process. From this standpoint the process has become an end in itself.

When, for example, their basic interest is affected, they are careful. They speak cautiously of an international conference. They say that it must be 'properly structured'. But we ask that the dialogue between ourselves and the Arabs of Eretz Yisrael under the auspices of the Americans will also be properly structured, making it impossible to submit any item to the agenda, that not just anyone, and certainly not terrorists, would be able to sit at the negotiating table.

But recently we have been quoted the famous saying of Dr. Henry Kissinger on 'constructive ambiguity'. I agree that at times diplomacy demands constructive ambiguity. Yet it must be said that sometimes there is a great danger of destructive ambiguity. It is at times desirable to use words as they are meant. And I will now do my best to use them.

The US government position towards the PLO hurts the chance to come to an agreement on two complementary levels: (a) the horrible, consistent, unreasonable, unexplained disregard of the responsibility of the PLO with all its factions for terrorist actions and the direct responsibility of the so-called moderate faction of the 'Fatah', to terrorist activity and the mute agreement for Arafat's terrorist veto on the residents of Judaea, Samaria and the Gaza district; and (b) the US stand as based on the clarifications which I have mentioned, affording the PLO a central role in the diplomatic process.

The conclusion drawn from this US position, on both planes, is distressing. Of course, our American friends and allies are an 'honest broker'. But if the US persists in this position towards the PLO, it will be extremely difficult for us to say that on this vital topic – the role, or rather non-role, of the PLO – the US is also an unprejudiced broker.

As for what we plan to do, maybe the day is near when, according to the time difference between Washington and

90

Jerusalem it is 'both day and night', and then it is possible that an unbridgeable gap will appear between the US position and the Cabinet decision of 5 November 1989. And therefore the assumption implicit in that decision, that the US is committed according to the Cabinet's points, will not be upheld. As such, members of the Labour Party, if this assumption is not upheld, neither can our agreement to the document containing the five points of Secretary of State Baker from 1 November 1989.

Under these conditions, if we follow the path that is the result of eagerness for negotiations at any price, there will be no negotiations – and we will pay the price.

We read in this week's Torah portion, 'Vayetze': 'And Yaakov went out from Be'er Sheva and went towards Haran ... and he dreamed and beheld a ladder set up on the earth and the top of it reached to heaven'. This is the way. Aspirations – yes; but feet on the ground – always. And thus, through an understanding of reality and of the constraints on this reality, with hope and sobriety, we can advance together with members of the Labour Party, and fulfil the responsibility placed upon us.

Speech before the Knesset, 13 December 1989

The Art of Non-Start

THE ART OF non-start, so typical of global diplomacy, has lately reached new levels that should surprise even veterans in the business of diplomatic mumbo-jumbo. Too often, foreign ministries are more interested in a diplomatic 'process' ('Let the hell something move there') than in the desired end-product of that elusive process. However, and especially in the intricate Middle East, process-oriented diplomacy, carried to the extreme, is plagued with self-defeating mechanisms that sooner, rather than later, will bring the 'process' mirage to an explosive end.

The Peace Initiative of the Shamir government of 14 May 1989 has presented a sincere, serious effort to reach a positive progress in the Arab–Israeli (or, rather the Islamic–Jewish) historic dispute. One of its four components is the proposal that the Arab inhabitants of Samaria, Judaea and the Gaza district will elect a delegation, with whom Israel will negotiate the arrangements for a transitional self-rule for the Arab inhabitants of these areas, in line with the Camp David compromise. The present difficulty is to name a small group of Arabs, residing in Judaea, Samaria and the Gaza district, with whom the procedures of these elections can be discussed and differences resolved.

The only hope for any progress lies in the possibility that, through the proposed elections, a local Arab leadership which is free from PLO or Hamas intimidation will emerge. This is exactly why the PLO would do its utmost to derail any attempt to implement the elections idea. This is exactly why those who really seek a positive movement, should do their utmost to exclude the PLO from the process altogether.

92

Regrettably, however, US clarifications to the PLO, as leaked in December 1989, include positions that disregard this consideration. The unavoidable conclusion is that the US assigns the PLO an important, even central, role in the diplomatic process.

This position stands in direct contrast to the basic guide-lines of 14 May 1989. In this context, the leaked draft response of Secretary Baker to the Israeli demand for as-surances embodied in the cabinet resolution of 5 November 1989, is especially alarming. It mentions that it is not the aim of the US *in this effort* to bring Israel into a dialogue or negotiations with the PLO. The combined leaks lead to a rational conclusion that, in the *next* effort, in the next stage, this *would* be the aim of the US.

It must be understood that PLO-nominated representa-tives, being free to sabotage the discussions, will use that opportunity to bog them down in a host of murky subjects which they will choose to include in the agenda. If such a loose framework is allowed, the chances that the proposed discussions will lead to an agreed procedure of elections are not poor – they are nil. Once the PLO is in, hope is out – which is why Mr Shamir has made it crystal-clear that if the PLO is in, Israel is out.

A process-oriented zeal is thus self-defeating. To be serious about the Israeli Peace Initiative means that you must seriously exclude from the process enemies of peace such as the PLO. Shrugging while mumbling (or vice versa): 'But what can we do, nothing can move without the PLO?' repre-sents a defeatist and dangerous approach. It is tantamount to declaring that nothing can move without the realization of the PLO's goals, which would lead to a Mid-Eastern 'peace'– with a non-existent, wiped-out State of Israel. As proposed in the past by Henry Kissinger, 'constructive ambiguity' in the wording of a diplomatic document is sometimes needed;

destructive ambiguity, however, must be avoided, and such language deleted, before it leads to disaster. The right timing for that is not difficult to define – it is now.

Therefore, to advance a fruitful process, Israel must receive a clear positive response to the assurances it requested from the US administration. Constructive clarity is obviously in great demand today.

Jerusalem Post, 9 February 1990

European Talks on Conventional Arms Limitations and their Ramifications for the Middle East

IN THE PAST few years the NATO allies in Europe and the United States have come to realize that the source of Europe's security problem is not nuclear weapons but the unacceptable disparity between the Warsaw Pact and NATO in conventional arms. In March 1989 23 European states, east and west, along with US Foreign Secretary Baker, gathered in Vienna for the first conference on conventional arms-limitation talks in Europe (CFE). What was the basis for the unacceptable disparity which needs correction? The figures presented in Vienna were simple. For example, if we take the parameter of tanks: 52,000 tanks in the Warsaw Pact against 22,000 in NATO – a ratio of 2.5 to 1 which is considered unreasonable and unacceptable to Western democracies.

I had the opportunity a few weeks ago to tell President Bush's US Ambassador to the conventional arms limitations talks in Vienna, Mr Lynn Hansen, that the significance of these talks transcends the question of European security. Why? Because now we have an opportunity to establish an agreed standard for reasonable national security.

95

The talks in Vienna are based upon two implicit guidelines: One, they resort to the infamous bean-counting method, irrespective of weapon sophistication. Thus, they do not insist that the sophistication of an American M-1 tank should be accounted for in comparison with its operationally equivalent Soviet T-72 tank. They do not say that. A simple count is taken.

According to the second principle, the enemy is judged by his capabilities, and not by his perceived intentions. This is why negotiations that began last March continue now, even after the dramatic collapse of the walls in Eastern Europe. Eastern Europeans are not told: 'Look, now that we are convinced that you are nice guys, if you want 52,000 tanks to play with, that's fine with us.' The requirement is still a 1:1 ratio between east and west armament: 20,000 tanks in the west must balance 20,000 tanks in the east, and the combined forces of East Germany, Czechoslovakia and Poland must not exceed 8000 tanks, against the same 8000 in the centre stage of Western Europe.

The new situation in Europe and the conventional arms limitations talks have a few immediate ramifications for the Middle East. First, with the expected cuts in NATO's security budget we must remain aware of the possibility that advanced western military technology will reach the Middle East, as an extension of the largely cynical attitude of Western Europe over the past decade. Secondly, we must also be aware of the possible arrival in the Middle East of advanced eastern military technology. The truth must be told: over the past few years the USSR has proven more responsible than the states of Western Europe in that it has greatly limited the deployment of first-line weapons in the Middle East. But now we hear of the Soviets' need for cash, which could push them to send first-line weapons to the Middle East for cash payment, indiscriminately.

We hear of another direct result – as we read in this week's newspaper – that the US has proposed the direct sale (if you can call it that) to Egypt, at a rock-bottom price, of hundreds of quite advanced, though not all modern, American M-60 tanks. It is not clear why Egypt needs hundreds of tanks when it has a peace accord with Israel, and with its improved ties with Libya. It should be expected that such a development will be mirrored by the Soviet bloc.

It is both possible and worthwhile to compare these new plausible standards of national security as defined for us by Europe in recent months, with the Middle East situation. We should examine whether we too can expect to enjoy a reasonable degree of national security, according to European concepts.

a. In terms of order-of-battle, on Israel's eastern front alone more than 12,000 tanks are deployed, compared with fewer than 4,000 in Israel, according to accepted publications. The ratio is therefore not 2.5 to 1, which is considered unacceptable in Europe, but is higher than 3 to 1.

b. Strategic depth: in Western Europe, which demands that no more than 20,000 tanks be emplaced opposite its central part, even its narrow section, opposite Holland and Belgium, is of some 300 miles. 'Greater Israel', however, from the Jordan to the Mediterranean Sea, opposite the metropolitan area of Tel Aviv, is only 45 miles wide.

c. Early warning: the current debate in NATO, is whether the standard warning time for NATO troops should be two weeks, as in the past, or four to six weeks. It is unnecessary to elaborate on the comparison to the need for early warning in our region, which is measured in days or hours.

d. Regimes: Surrounding us are dictatorships which show no sign of collapse in the near future. We still have not witnessed an Arab, say a Syrian, poet gather half a million

97

Syrians in the Damascus Square and call to replace the dictatorship with democracy. The first experiment in democracy in 23 years, in the Hashemite Kingdom in Jordan – and here I join the assertion of Minister of Defence Rabin that we must aim at the stabilization of this kingdom because its proposed alternatives are certainly worse – this first democratic experiment has resulted in a Jordanian Parliament comprising some 40 per cent Muslim fundamentalists.

e. The frequency and intensity of wars: Since the worst of all wars ended 45 years ago, Europe has not seen a war, while the Middle East in the past decade alone has known the horrors of the Iran-Iraq war and its one million casualties. From the point of view of intentions, the most accurate recent account of the current Arab nations' intention is the concluding declaration made on 26 May 1989 at the Casablanca summit just two weeks after the announcement of Israel's peace initiative. It included the Arab commitment to 'the right of return', and to the rallying of all Arab power to achieve strategic parity to contain 'Israeli aggression'.

This comparison leads to the following conclusions. Externally, we should say, as I do in my meetings with representatives of Europe and the US, that we are not spoiled. Every day we pay a certain price for having chosen to establish the Jewish State in Eretz Yisrael, in the Middle East and not in Birobidjan, in Uganda or in Argentina. We are not spoiled, but we demand of our friends in the US and in Europe the application of the same standards of national security which they seek to apply to their children.

We must also pressure our European and American friends to pressure, in turn, the Arab countries to meet us at the diplomatic table for peace talks without prior conditions. In the last few months we have been told, 'Speak with the PLO'. Why? Because you must speak with your enemy. We have not heard that this pressure is being exerted on Syria, on Jordan, or on Iraq, a country with which we have no apparent territorial dispute.

Internally, in view of these data, we must retain a constant recognition of the necessity to retain the Israel Defence Force's ability to withstand these concrete threats. I say this also in answer to the recurring demands for ongoing cuts in the defence budget. To some, this sometimes contrasts with the need for funds to settle new olim. Thank God, there will be hundreds of thousands of olim. The State of Israel will have to protect them too, in the safe haven which it established for the Jewish nation worldwide.

Therefore, in conclusion, when it is suggested to us that we should learn from what has happened these past few months in Eastern Europe, I think it is worthwhile for the Knesset to discuss the entire scene in Europe, its ramifications for the Middle East and specifically for the State of Israel.

Speech before the Knesset, 21 February 1990

The Water Divide

THE CHAIRMAN OF the Labour Party, Mr Shimon Peres, appeared a few months ago before a forum of European parliamentaries and their Israeli colleagues, explaining that Israel opposes an independent Arab state west of the Jordan River because Israelis do not accept an Arab army at the gates of Jerusalem. This statement, he was told after the discussion, may be interpreted that Israel would agree to the establishment of an independent Arab state with no such army. But that is not the intention, Mr Peres responded, and went on his way.

Where is Mr Peres headed, or rather, where is he being led? His deputy, Member of Knesset Beilin, proclaimed from the Knesset podium in direct contradiction of the government position that he and his party await the green light from PLO headquarters in Tunis. However, Mr Peres did not wait, and through the services of the Weizmann (Jerusalem)–Tibi (Tunis) duo, tried to operate the traffic light and cause the PLO gang to provide the expected approval. This is what Mr Peres calls 'movement'.

In the public debate on the composition of an Arab delegation for diplomatic talks to implement the Israeli government's peace initiative, attention has been drawn away from the Labour Party heads' trickery of the general public and specifically of their traditional supporters. They simply take the old slogans and apply them to a framework totally divorced from the original source. Let us remember that 20 years ago two assumptions were proposed by the Labour Party: substantial areas of Samaria, Judaea, and the Gaza district are part of our homeland, yet must be viewed as bargaining chips in talks with the Hashemite Kingdom, chips that would be given to the Hashemites in return for a peace treaty with Israel. In the 20 years following the spring of 1967 the Labour Party has attempted to sell its stillborn scheme to the public, as if an Arab ruler would be interested, or able, to sign a peace treaty with Israel transferring 'holy Arab land' west of the Jordan River, including Jerusalem, to Jewish sovereignty.

When King Hussein, in his summer 1988 speech, made it clear that the Labour Party's scheme is detached from reality, they remained with a slogan without an address. Yet they did not abandon the slogan, and merely changed the address: today they seek 'territorial compromise' with representatives of the Arab residents of Samaria, Judaea and the Gaza district. But it is not only the address that has been changed. Labour Party leaders have altered their attitude towards the territorial bargaining chips. While continuing to wave them in the air, they announce in every possible forum that they are doing so because they burn their fingers. It is not viable, they say, or even possible, or nice or moral to hold the 'territories' for a long period of time. It is strange that those politicians expect that with such statements they can obtain a reasonable price for their merchandise in the Middle East bazaar.

The past months have seen repeated shrugging, accompanied by the statement, 'What can we do – the PLO is the dominant factor in the area?'. This being the case, it can be concluded that the proposed 'territorial compromise' is with this 'dominant factor'. From this one can deduce the logical assumption: according to the confused Labour Party, in the best possible scenario, Israel evacuates most of Samaria, Judaea and the Gaza district, and in these areas the ruler will be none other than 'the dominant factor in the area'. What will this 'dominant factor', the PLO, do with these evacuated areas? It can be assumed that the PLO will establish an independent, democratic secular Arab state as Stage 1 in its multi-phased plan.

The Labour Party's platform for the twelfth Knesset was drafted after a year of Arab violence commonly termed 'intifada'. Its authors, to whom Woodrow Wilson's idea of self-determination is not foreign, none the less decided to include a section clearly opposing the establishment of an independent Arab state west of the Jordan. The man in the street may thereby conclude that in their opinion a PLO state is a real threat to the very existence of the Jewish state. In the light of this logical analysis, one can only ask the confused Labour Party leaders with a Jewish sigh: 'Nu?'!

Based on these considerations, the political water divide within the Israeli public is being defined, between those who comprehend the horrifying significance of the establishment of a twenty-second Arab state in Western Eretz Yisrael, and those who are willing to accept the fateful results of this diplomatic process. The latter demand that this process begin immediately with no pre-conditions, no 'dealing with pettiness', in the broad-minded words of the Labour Party chairman; that is, by way of surrendering to the 'petty demands' of Arafat. A delegation which would include one or two deportees to represent the Palestinian Arab diaspora, which would demand the right of return to Jaffa? That's not too bad, and even good – the circle will be enlarged, and the more the merrier. A delegation that would include one or two Arab representatives from Jerusalem? That's not too bad, and even good – Jerusalem will immediately become an issue on the diplomatic table, and the controversy will be clarified. The proposed delegation is a reward for those who provoke the intifada? That's not too bad, and even good – with whom can we speak if not with them? After all, the 'Hamas' is worse than the 'Unified Command'. The Likud opposes all of this?

That is not bad, and even good – the PLO will agree and that, after all, is what counts.

Nonsense. We must reiterate to those who, in the muddle of scripts and scenarios, parameters and analyses, telephones and facsimiles, prefer to forget that the PLO, with all its factions, is an umbrella organization of active murderous gangs. The PLO, with all its factions, has one clear goal: the destruction of the State of Israel. The PLO, with most of its factions, strives to achieve this aim in stages. The PLO, with all its factions, are the enemies of peace, and therefore their participation in the diplomatic process, directly or indirectly, means relinquishing hope for achieving agreement with the Arab residents of Samaria, Judaea and the Gaza district.

The Labour Party's continuous withdrawal from its own positions has a significant effect on the United States' evasive answers to Israel's demand for a clear positive response to the assurances it requested in the Israeli Cabinet decision of 5 November 1989. This decision is an important criterion to test the political conditions to be expected at the opening of talks on the Israeli government's peace initiative. Under the unfolding conditions, maybe we should refrain from entering a destructive diplomatic process today, in order to achieve the desired settlement in the future.

Jerusalem Post, 25 February 1990

The US Position
Towards PLO

THE LEADERS of the PLO reiterate their position that without East Jerusalem as the capital of the independent Palestinian state, without recognition of the PLO and the realization of the right of the Palestinian diaspora to return to Jaffa and to Haifa, there can be no peace. Our doves are then humming, 'Words, just words, there is no reason to get excited over words; we must judge the PLO not by its words but by its deeds'. Let us, then, judge the PLO by its deeds.

I am holding in my hand a map which was found in the pocket of PLO terrorists, members of Hawatmah's 'Democratic Front for the Liberation of Palestine' (DFLP). They were killed on their way from Lebanon to Israel on 26 January, just two months ago. The map shows the PLO-planned route, crossing the Litani River, across the village of Taiba where they were killed. The border fence is marked, as well as their destination: Kibbutz Misgav Am. Another detail, belonging to PLO-Hawatmah, the fifth this year, was eliminated last week before reaching their target, the village of Zar'it.

I ask you to examine the following facts: PLO-Hawatmah, the 'Democratic Front for the Liberation of Palestine', continue to perpetrate acts of terror against Israel's citizens, while Hawatmah's second-in-command, Yassir Abed-Rabu, heads the PLO delegation for talks with the US in Tunisia. Not only do we understand the ramifications of these facts but the US State Department also understands them, yet refuses to reach the proper conclusions.

Two days ago, the State Department submitted to the chairman of the Senate Foreign Relations Committee, Senator Claybourne Pell, its report on PLO compliance with its commitment to renounce terrorism. This report is a somewhat positive step towards revealing the truth of PLO terrorism, yet it does not go nearly far enough.

On 12 July 1989 Mr John Kelly, US Under-secretary of State, testified before the House Sub-committee on Europe and Middle Eastern affairs. Between the opening of the talks with the PLO and the day of his testimony, three attacks were executed by PLO-Hawatmah in February and March 1989, and one by the 'Islamic Jihad' on 15 March. The 'Islamic Jihad', as we all know, is part of the larger mechanism of the Eastern sector, the major operational arm of the 'Fatah'. The 'Fatah' commander, 'Abu-Amar', is more commonly known as Yasser Arafat.

Indeed, the report is a partial admittance of the July mistake, yet owing to the scarcity of details, the covering up of facts, and the unfounded conclusions, the report is an unsuccessful, pathetic attempt to cover up for the PLO, to camouflage its terrorist nature in an effort to legitimize the terror syndicate in order to find an excuse to continue the dialogue with it.

I shall now present an example. The US report notes the attack by the DFLP on 2 March, in which four terrorists were killed and one escaped, in the Lebanon security zone. The report presents the DFLP's announcement accepting responsibility for the attack and detailing its target – the village of Zar'it. Yet the report's authors outrageously point out that this target is not clear. How could they possibly reach such a clear conclusion about such a blurred target?

According to the report, the Americans checked all three incidents with the PLO in Tunis. The PLO representative in these talks is deputy chief of the Democratic Front, Yasser Abed-Rabu. Maybe we are expected to fail to protect our

105

towns so that PLO terror will cause civilian casualties, so that these reports can clearly state that the target is, in fact, the murder of men, women and children.

So much for the few acts of terror that have been singled out by the US report. But numerous terrorist activities by the PLO are not mentioned at all in the report, which is updated to at least 5 February 1990. By 15 December 1988, the number of PLO attacks against Israel was 30, not nine. Of these, 17 attacks occurred outside Israel's borders, two by the 'Fatah', and 13 in Israel within the 'green line', by the Fatah details of Force-17. Although these are known to the American Administration, the US Secretary of State assured Congress on 1 March, just three weeks ago, that 'the PLO adheres to its commitment to refrain from terror'.

The report reiterates this unfounded conclusion, adding that 'one problem area has been some actions undertaken by Damascus-based PLO groups such as the PFLP and DFLP. We have no evidence that these actions were authorized or approved by the PLO Executive Committee or Arafat person-ally'. Really. Of course the execution of attacks is not authorized through a proper process by the PLO Executive Committee – the terrorist mechanisms of the PLO are in charge of these actions. Within the 'Fatah' these are: the Hawari mechanism, the Western sector and Force-17. The commander of Force-17, Abu-Taib, one of Arafat's closest aides, is in charge of his personal protection. It is, of course, a cynical pretence to claim that PLO leaders, including Arafat himself, are not associated with the incessant terror.

With this background, it is understandable why the report's authors chose to ignore the Fatah's action completely – I repeat, the *Fatah* action, I repeat again, the Fatah action – in the Mount Hariff area in the Negev, on 4 December 1989; five terrorists with 50 hand grenades, on their way to an indiscriminate massacre.

Why? After all, the Americans are our friends, our allies, and generally they are generous and fair people. Why have they recently adopted a new version of the carrot-and-stick method – a carrot to the PLO, the stick to Israel? Why have they made an effort to compose such a pathetic report, blurring most of the footprints leading from the terror attacks to the PLO leadership? The answer lies in the past year's American foreign policy: a political process at any price.

During this past year two tenets that led the shapers of US foreign policy have been refuted: (a) against their expectations, the PLO has so far refused to accept a secondary, latent role in the process; and (b) against their hopes, the PLO continues its tradition of murderous terror since its inception in 1964. The US State Department hoped that the terror would stop, if not totally then at least the 'Fatah' would halt its operations; that if 'Fatah' would continue its terror, at least it would not operate in that part of Israel west of the 'green line'; that if it would operate in Israel at least it would not be against civilians. All of these calculations were made without consulting the boss, and the boss in the PLO murder syndicate is Yasser Arafat.

Despite all this, the US State Department intends to continue talks with the PLO. They try to purify the sin and when unsuccessful, they turn the tables of logic around: rather than demanding the termination of all terrorist actions as the basis for continuing talks with the PLO, they hint that because of the PLO's ability to place a terrorist veto on the political process, we must speak with them. Not despite the terror which it exerts but because of it, because nowadays they consider the PLO the 'major factor in the area'.

This is terrible logic, a horrifying submission to murder and intimidation. According to this, the more monstrous the PLO is – or, in the words of MK Zucker in the Knesset a month ago, the PLO is not even beastly, as 'beasts do not

107

destroy their own' – the need to include them in the political process will grow. Woe to the eyes that see such distorted logic.

Let us ask again: how can we complain about our American friends? The Israeli Labour Party, in accepting the logic of the radical left, also accepted this flawed method in its haste to detach itself from Samaria, Judaea and the Gaza district. And this is how today the Labour Party sees the PLO not as an obstacle but as a tool that will allow it to return more or less to the old, familiar, pleasant 'green line', behind the infamous electronic fence. This is how, before our eyes, a new, 'improved' humanistic left is emerging, one that does not demand cessation from terror as a condition for talking to the PLO, that is ready to live with terror, explaining why we must give in to terrorism and why it is worth our while to negotiate with its instigators.

And therefore, the then Deputy Finance Minister, MK Yossi Beilin, said on 24 January of this year: 'We in the Government felt that the factor that might influence the PLO to give the "green light" to the Palestinians in the territories to negotiate with us about elections is America.' And he continued: 'As our purpose is clearly to cause the PLO to be the factor that accepts our political plan and who will give the "green light" to the Palestinians in the territories to negotiate with us in order to reach elections.' Thus the Peres–Weizman–Tibi–Tunis axis was established, as testified by the pivotal player, Ezer Weizman. And yesterday, MK Peres rushed to inform the Egyptian nation, in an interview with *El-Ahram*, that his government, when formed, will change the law forbidding meetings with the PLO. A 'green light' you seek from these murderers, who continue to kill on their two-staged way to eradicate Israel.

In a sugary article in the latest edition of *Foreign Policy*, entitled 'Lowering the Sword', Arafat's deputy Salah Halef, or Abu Iyad, brought the following words of peace:

A Palestinian state in East Jerusalem, the West Bank, and Gaza may not be sufficient in itself to solve the problem of millions of Palestinian refugees living in subhuman camps around the Arab world, and the Palestinian issue will continue to undermine peace in the Middle East until the problem of the Palestinian diaspora is settled. We must therefore insist that the 'right to return' should be on the agenda of any negotiation for the settlement of the Palestinian-Israeli conflict.

With regard to this, our doves are cooing: 'It's merely rhetoric, no cause for alarm. We will test the PLO by its deeds.' This is exactly what we have done the past few minutes, and the results are conclusive: terror, murder, and more terror.

The Labour Party, who accept the lack of logic in American policy over the past months, who want negotiations without restrictions, without assurances, should heed the words read last week in the Book of Esther: 'For if you remain quiet in this time, salvation for the Jews will come from another place.'

Knesset Session, 21 March 1990

US Hesitations to Halt Talks with the PLO

ON A HARRIED and bitter winter night of 1988, the US government opened the sluice-gates to a muddy flood by opening negotiations, 'substantive dialogue', with the PLO in Tunis. Over the course of the months and weeks which have passed since this tragic, maybe historic mistake, our American partners have continued to tell me: 'Our intentions, as well as our deeds, are desirable; we intend to tame the beast'. I repeatedly answered: 'Sooner or later – apparently sooner – you will realize that the beast has tamed you.'

We were not so wrong, according to the recent events, and ample proof that it is indeed so came with the US State Department's presentation before Congress on 19 March 1990, reporting on the extent of the correlation between the PLO's commitment to abstain from terrorism and its actual behaviour. This House has already discussed the report, a whitewashing account, camouflaging and concealing, a report that proves that if riding a tiger is dangerous riding a hyena stinks.

Three weeks have passed since the PLO-Abu-el-Abas operation on Israel's beaches which was intended to be a mass murder. Since then, on the issue of talks between the US and the PLO, the American administration still considers and weighs, thinks and ponders, hesitates and appeals, questions and vacillates. And vacillates, and vacillates. What signal do these vacillations give to the leaders of terrorists and other crazies around the world? What do such hesitations signal to the Arab states?

Of all possible questions, I would like to address the honourable minister representing the government the following question: After the attempted attack by the PLO-Abu-el-Abas, initial reports showed that the US Embassy in Tel-Aviv was one of the terrorists' targets. My question to the minister is two-fold: A. Has further clarification of the PLO-Abu-el-Abas operation shown that indeed the US embassy was one of the targets planned in the attack? B. If the US embassy in Tel-Aviv was in fact a target of the terrorist plans, is this known to the US administration?

We were not mistaken in our basic position. It was wrong from the outset, both morally and practically, to establish contact with the murder syndicate of the PLO. Because even according to those who adopt a lighter approach, who said that the PLO is under probation, who say that it will be examined through its deeds and not through its statements – it is clear to them also, that the PLO has completely failed the test which they had devised for it, an awful, bloody failure.

In contrast to some expectations that I had until this morning, I have to tell MK Sarid that you have disappointed me. You turned to me on an important issue, a different one, on the pages of the newspaper a few weeks ago. You called upon me: 'Stand up, you brave fellow, and express your opinion on that issue' (and, of course, I would not like to compare it or even mention it). After your party's statement following the attack on the Shavuot holiday, in which you said that if Arafat cannot find a way to get rid of the killer Abu-el-Abas he will be tied in with that attack, what conclusion have you reached today?

I am almost tempted to call upon you: Stand up, you brave fellow, and express your opinion, and demand that the American government reach the conclusion imminent in

111

your words – that it is impossible to continue with these contacts. But I think that my own conclusion is that after a year and a half in this House I still have much to learn.

We therefore demand that our American friends adopt a serious approach to the peace process. If their administration's policy on the issue of peace in our area is indeed serious, they should prove it in two ways: A. by halting the shameful talks with leaders of the PLO murder syndicate, in Tunis or anywhere else; and B. by serious study of the issue of peace and the attempt to understand that the relations between Jews and Arabs west of the Jordan River are only one single issue, important as it may be, on the agenda. The major problem threatening peace in the Middle East is the relationship between the Jewish State and the immediate surrounding Arab states and their neighbours – states which hate, which arm and threaten, and which have already attempted to realize their destructive plans.

This two-track approach, which deals with a comprehensive peace in the Middle East, is well anchored in the Camp David Accords. He who abandons the comprehensive approach for the policy aimed at ending Israeli control of Samaria, Judaea and the Gaza district, is exposing the State of Israel to a danger to its very existence.

Our approach to the question at issue is a serious one. We have proven this in the past, at the time of signing the Camp David Accords and at the time of their implementation. The central concept of the Camp David Accords is the Israeli concept. It was brought to Camp David by a relative of mine who is also, through my sister, related to the minister who responds today on behalf of the government. The wisdom of Camp David holds that it is our duty to approach the issue gradually, by means of an interim agreement. It is ironic that specifically the agreement to transfer Taba to Egyptian rule practically prevents any Arab leadership today from reaching

112

an agreement with us on the basis of what is called 'territorial compromise'. After the Egyptians gained control of the last grain of what they consider sacred Arab soil, where in the near future is an Arab leadership which will agree to less than that? Therefore the wisdom of Camp David is still valid: we have to move gradually, by means of an interim agreement.

I would like to state clearly what will probably not be pleasant to some members of the coalition. The Camp David Accords are open-ended toward the future, completely open. We do not try, at the opening of negotiations or through them, to force upon the Arabs what they cannot accept. These accords are open. In the first stage we will speak of an interim period. We shall be dealing with the future status of Samaria, of Judaea and the Gaza district, but we are not telling the Arabs, 'Join us in negotiations during the interim period, but we are telling you ahead of time that you will be barred from raising your claim for sovereignty in these disputed areas'. We do not say this.

We have also proved our serious intent during the negotiations, which were halted by the Egyptians in 1982. We agreed, in accordance with our proposal, that the administrative council would be granted broad authority in all areas. The draft of the proposed agreement of 1982 is still on the table.

I hold that original document – the proposed powers for the administrative council in thirteen areas – and with the Speaker's permission I will read three of them:

1. Administration of Justice; 3. Finance, including taxation; 11. Local Police, including maintenance of prisons for criminal offenders sentenced by the courts in the areas. And these are just a few examples.

We are serious in our position. It is less important that our seriousness be proved to our friends across the ocean. It is more important that our Arab neighbours here will read the documents, analyse them, reject the illusion that violence will force us to make the further-reaching offer – that we shall commit ourselves to the future establishment of the twenty-second Arab state –, reject that clown that heads the PLO terror syndicate, who in Geneva waved a 2000 year-old coin in support of his claim. They should sit with us on the basis of these proposals, for their own future and for the futures of Arab and Jewish children in Eretz Yisrael.

Speech before the Knesset, 20 June 1990

Extending a Hand

THE ARAB DRUMS of war, amplified by the media, cause some to approach the Middle East in a manner similar to that of parents 'resolving' a family feud. Their younger son, a real brat, steals the ball from his older brother. The latter insists on having the ball back; the little brat cries; the older one shouts; Mum and Dad rush in, yelling at him: 'Can't you behave like an adult?! Let him have it at once.' 'But listen, listen –', insists the poor kid. 'No buts,' they retort, 'We don't want to hear about it any more. Just give him that silly thing.' And they return to the living-room.

Paying a price for being reasonable can be a painful experience. Saddam Hussein stays high and dry: as an infamous butcher he is no address for useless scolding. The Syrians, expanding into Lebanon, and insisting on the Golan Heights (a tiny fraction of their 185,680 sq. km country), are no client for fruitless admonishing. Therefore it has been concluded that 'our Israeli friends', 'those nice people', should be the target for anger and frustration, and are put to a grotesque test of their seriousness towards peace.

'But –', we try to tell our friends, 'Listen. Please listen.' Twelve years ago – long before the current phase of Arab violence in Samaria, the Galilee, Judaea, Jerusalem and the Gaza district – it was we who initiated the one and only practical proposal which has any merit and stands any chance. Many are aware of it. Few really understand it.

Last week I was surprised to learn that even some of my seasoned colleagues in the Knesset are not fully aware of the significance of the Camp David accords. In my motion for the agenda I urged our friends to involve themselves in a serious, in-depth attempt to understand that Arab-Jewish relations west of the Jordan River is just one item – however important – on the agenda. The main issue threatening Middle East peace is the relationship between the Jewish State and its immediate neighbouring Arab states, and their neighbours, which hate, arm, threaten, and which in the past have tried to implement their plots.

This two-track approach, dealing with comprehensive peace in the Middle East, is clearly anchored in the Camp David Accords. Abandoning this all-encompassing approach while declaring that the political goal is to end the Israeli occupation of Samaria, Judaea, and the Gaza district, exposes the State of Israel to a threat to its very existence.

The Camp David Accords are totally open-ended towards the future. We are not asking, at the outset of the talks or upon their continuation, to impose on the Arabs anything they are not willing to accept. We are dealing with the future sovereignty of Samaria, Judaea, and the Gaza district. We are not telling the Arabs: Come and talk with us on the interim period, but you will never be able to raise your claim to sovereignty on these disputed areas. We do not say that.

... We have proven our seriousness within the negotiations which were stopped by the Egyptians at the beginning of 1982. We agreed, according to our proposals, that the Administrative Council will enjoy broad powers in every realm. The draft agreement which we proposed in 1982 is still on the table. I am holding the original document – the powers offered to the Administrative Council are in thirteen different fields, three of which are: 1. Administration of justice; 3. Finance, including taxation; 11. Local police, including maintenance of prisons for criminal offenders sentenced by the courts in the area.

We are serious in our position. It is less important that our seriousness be demonstrated to our friends beyond the sea. It is more important that our Arab neighbours here will realize it, will read the documents, will examine them, will forsake the illusion that violence will force us to offer them more far-reaching proposals – that we shall commit ourselves to the establishment of the twenty-second Arab state in the future – and detach themselves from that clown heading the PLO murder syndicate, who waved in Geneva a 2000-year-old coin to support his position.

Let them sit with us at the table on the basis of these proposals for our future, for our sake, for their sake, for their future, for the future of Arab and Jewish children in Eretz Yisrael.

The foregoing may not be the slickest presentation of the concept, I simply believe in what I say. I mean it, and we in the Likud mean it. Our responsibility to offer a peaceful solution to our Arab neighbours stems from our basic approach towards Eretz Yisrael. We mean business – this is a serious proposal.

Jerusalem Post, 29 June 1990

Retaining Israel's Qualitative Edge

THE IRAQI AIR Force comprises some 700 combat aircraft. It is the sole target of the US Air Force and Navy, which have deployed in the Gulf area more than 800 combat aircraft, 500 of them first-line sophisticated machines: F-14s, 15s, 16s, 18s, 111s and 117s. This order-of-battle, and this ratio of forces, may serve as a yardstick against which the challenge of the Israeli Air Force can be judged. Having to deal with 1800 combat airplanes of Iraq, Syria, Jordan, Saudi Arabia and Libya, the IAF employs only about 600, of which only some 200 are modern, quality air machines.

How do we do it, then? How are we to survive in the treacherous, savage Mid-Eastern environment, while so out-numbered? Well, of course, through our 'Qualitative Edge'. 'You can do it', we are told, 'because you are smart'. Though compliments are always a pleasure to hear, winning a war through compliments becomes an increasingly difficult task.

As long as Israel employed top-line weapon systems many years before its enemies acquired them, Qualitative Edge was a concrete and meaningful term. However, recently our enemies have been supplied with the most sophisticated weapons. The Soviets, who traditionally used to be more cautious, now sell the Arab countries first-line aircraft such as MiG-29 and Suhoy-24; the Western Europeans supply them with weapons such as Roland anti-aircraft missiles or the Gazelle attack helicopter; and now the United States.

In recent years, the US has been selling Arab countries

first-line weapon systems such the F-18, F-16 and F-15, and recently also modern Patriot anti-aircraft batteries. But now we have entered into a new era, in which the US is ready to sell our enemies some weapons which Israel does not have, such as Multi-Launcher-Rocket Systems and TOW-2A anti-tank missiles. With the newly proposed arms sale to Saudi Arabia a new stage has been attained: not only line-one weapons are to be sold, but even a 'line-zero' system – the M1-A2 tank which has not been manufactured yet and which even the US Army would not field in the near future. Where, then, is the Israeli Qualitative Edge?

So it's not easy. Being juxtaposed between Iraq, Syria and Libya is difficult enough, and with so much instability around, we surely do not need an eroding Israeli deterrence as an add-on destabilizer. As flying-by-wire in Arabic cannot be all that different from flying-by-wire in Hebrew, to have such sophisticated tools in the hands of Jihadists, who vow to use them against the Jewish State, is very troubling indeed. Something must be done, so that the US commitment to Israel's Qualitative Edge does not hang there, as a shabby poster, occasionally flapping against the wall, producing some noises but not very useful.

The way is clear: Israel must be able to produce its own secret weapons, so that it can really surprise its enemies once they wage a new holy war against it. To be able to do that, two things must happen: (a) some basic technologies that have been inaccessible to Israel should be opened, and (b) a mechanism should be determined that would allow Israel to invest more Israeli currency in its own weapon industry. In other words, instead of only 25 per cent of the US military aid being converted to Israeli shekels today, we should aim at a substantially higher sum. With the new, enormous arms sales to Saudi Arabia, such an arrangement should not adversely affect the US industry.

In addition, a new R&D co-operation package should be implemented, allowing Israeli and American weapon companies to enter into advanced joint projects. With shrinking US defence budgets and the pressing need for smarter weapons, Israel can contribute many bright ideas, with a relatively low-cost R&D and a quick-response cycle with the actual field requirements from which both countries could benefit.

Israel will never ask for American troops to defend it, either before or after any Christmas. We do, though, follow Churchill's formula in the early 1940s, when Britain stood alone against enemies of the civilized democracies: 'Give us the tools and we shall do the job'.

Jerusalem Post, December 1990

A Brave New
Diplomacy

THE NEW alignment in the Middle East is being extensively discussed, as the Iraqi military machine is being intensively destroyed. New opportunities open up, but new threats evolve. Renewal of extremist, anti-Israel Arab nationalism can be expected; and violent Islamic fundamentalism is still on the rise, with King Hussein sitting on a shaky throne 80 kilometres east of Jerusalem.

Last week, in his testimony before the House Foreign Affairs Committee, Secretary of State James Baker raised some questions pertaining to a meaningful peace process in the Middle East. He asked: 'What is the best diplomatic vehicle for getting the process under way?' The best vehicle is, not surprisingly, the Framework for Peace in the Middle East as agreed at Camp David in 1978.

It has become a habit to neglect the fact that the Framework (and therefore also the Israeli peace initiative of 14 May 1989) deals not only with the relations between Jews and Arabs west of the Jordan River, but requires the broadening of the scope of peace to include Arab states. More effort should now be devoted to the latter aspect, as more rigorous treatment is needed here.

For too long, we have been exposed to the guessing game of who means what, when he says this or that; and therefore we certainly need an accurate, simple and obvious litmus test. The following two questions should be directed, on a one-to-one basis, to the Arab leaders who consider themselves to be in a state of war with Israel:

- Do you unequivocally accept the natural right of the Jewish People to establish and maintain a viable Jewish State in the Land of Israel (Palestine can also be used, if it helps)?
- Are you ready to enter face-to-face, open, bilateral negotiations, without prior conditions, aimed at the conclusion of a contractual peace treaty with the Jewish State of Israel (just Israel can also be used, if it helps)?

Any leader in the Free World would see no difficulty in responding positively to these questions. But we should not be surprised if Arab leaders would have a hard time responding similarly. However, until a clear, short, positive answer to this questionnaire is obtained, not too much can be expected from a new Pax Americana as it relates to the Arab–Israeli (or, rather, the Muslim–Jewish) state of belligerency.

Despite the prospect of receiving evasive or even negative answers, the leaders of the new, emerging world can be expected to insist on positive answers to both these questions. General terms such as Peace and Reconciliation, as found in the Baker–Bessmertnykh joint declaration, are important and useful, but they fall short of clearly needed concrete terms. 'If you are serious about peace' (to use a Mr Baker classic), this approach should be adopted as a new diplomatic standard.

Mr Baker added another question last week, asking 'How will regional arms control arrangements affect this process?'

I would suggest that the question be reversed. It is the 'meaningful process', as suggested above, that should affect the arrangements, and not vice versa. The reason is the awkward fact that the Middle East is different from the European theatre.

In the Israeli situation, the basic long-term threat is not

miscalculation; it is cool, cruel, systematic and difficult-to-deter Calculation, aimed at the elimination of the Jewish democracy from the heart of the Arab Nation. Until this element is openly eliminated from Middle East politics, arms-control arrangements will be of little use, or even detrimental.

Because the basic issue of the legitimacy of a specific state in Europe does not exist, a bottom-up approach was workable there. But in the Middle East, where Israel is still generally considered illegitimate, a top-to-bottom approach must logically be applied.

The American APS (Acronym Production Syndrome) has produced 'CBM', for Confidence-Building Measures. These are very important diplomatic tools, but they must be used only within the context of a well-defined process, its declared goal being the conclusion of peace treaties with Israel. From my point of view as an Israeli, a Pax Americana which virtually excludes Israel is not a very interesting project.

A new political alignment in this armed, violent, Jew-hating part of the world must be accompanied by a re-aligned state of mind on the part of the Arab leadership. With the failure of 'constructive ambiguity', 'constructive clarity' should now be used, and the US can play a major role in achieving that goal if it adopts a brave, new diplomacy.

Jerusalem Post, 15 February 1991

Strategic Depth Still Counts

'MISSILES ARE not too impressed by "strategic depth". When a missile is launched from Iraq or Syria it does not stop in Judaea, in Samaria or in the Gaza district in order to receive permission to continue on its course.' This statement, heard recently among leaders of the Israeli left, is intended to undermine the assumption that Israeli rule over the area west of the Jordan River is vital to the existence of the Jewish State. The smart wording cannot hide the superficial thought behind the left's policy.

Even after the Arab missile attack on Israel's population centres, it must be understood that the source of the threat to Israel's existence is a ground attack, and a missile attack only increases this threat. In support of this thesis I refer to the important conclusion reached by the Jaffee Center for Strategic Studies, in its 1988 report, referring to the possibility that an independent Arab state would be created west of the Jordan, devoid of heavy weaponry.

Among the dangers to Israel as enumerated in this report, the central one is that 'the temptation would be great for Arab ground forces, employing armour and artillery, to seize Judaea and Samaria, completing the first stage in a single night's movement from the Jordan bridges to the Israeli border'.

We face here the common military problem of calculating 'time and space'. The State of Israel will always be protected by a small standing army, dependent on its reserves, and will always require a process to mobilize these reserves. The mobilization will always take a few days, and can be executed only after the warning, assessment, deliberation and decision by a democratic government. This is the practical timetable that should be compared to the above assumption, that a few hours are sufficient for a large Arab land force to be deployed at a zero distance from our population centre, the strategic centre of the State of Israel.

The problem of missiles exacerbates this danger. The Syrian Army has fielded accurate missiles with a range of 100 kilometres, as well as missiles with a range of 300 kilometres, carrying conventional warheads weighing 1,000 kilograms, and even carrying chemical warheads. Chinese missiles with a range of 2,500 kilometres were supplied to Saudi Arabia and could reach Iranian hands.

In a coordinated attack, our enemies can inflict serious damage to our airfields, using their accurate missiles, and inflict heavy casualties to population centres, using the others. This would disrupt Israel's ability to maintain the vital mobilization of its reserves, while a large ground force crosses the Jordan, greeted by the Arab residents cheering on their rooftops in demilitarized Samaria, reaching the heart of Israel 'in a single night's movement'. This is a severe-yet-plausible scenario, and its potential realization carries the serious and not-improbable ramification: the surrender of the Jewish State.

It is not necessary to be a member of the Knesset Foreign Affairs and Defence Committee to reach the conclusion that the threat to Israel's existence is indeed a group attack from the east.

Examination of the Labour Party's platform reveals this recognition in its keystone item, stressing that Israel's 'security border' (however hazy this term may be) must be the Jordan River. Yet, if anyone postulates in the wake of the Gulf War, that 'a missile from Iraq or Syria will not stop in Judaea, in Samaria or in the Gaza district in order to request permission to continue on its path', it must be understood that such a missile will not stop to present a passport at Israeli outposts along the Jordan River. And this even if the Jordan Valley is under Israeli sovereignty, according to the concept of 'territorial compromise'.

Relinquishing parts of Judaea and Samaria would immediately lead to a single possible result: the seizing of power by a mixture of the PLO and Hamas, and the establishment of a terrorist Arab state. The danger in its constitution is its ability to mobilize the Arab force, using the slogan of Arab solidarity in order to implement the Arab 'right to return' to Jaffa and Lod.

If there is no strategic value to the Samarian hills and the Judaean mountains, it is impossible to assign a real security value to meagre forces deployed along the narrow strip of the Jordan Valley, in a topographically inferior area. These troops would find themselves caught between the pincers of an Arab army invading from the east and an enemy state at their west, while the mobilization of reserves would be interrupted by missile attacks. This 'security' proposal, adopted by the Labour Party for the past 24 years, stands in direct contrast to the basic military rule: there can be no defence without depth, and there is no meaning to 'depth' without a territorial continuity to the strategic centre.

If there is no strategic value to the hills of Samaria and Judaea, it is difficult to see what strategic meaning the Israeli left attributes to the plains of the Golan Heights. If the guideline is 'compromise at any price,' it is to be expected that the Golan Heights would be included in that price. According to the new line of thought, Syrian missiles will not stop to request permission to pass over Kibbutz Marom Golan, and therefore the 'strategic depth' will be provided by 'peace arrangements' with Hafez Assad or his brother Rifat.

Leaders of the left have refrained these past few years, and not coincidentally, from demanding the pursuit of peace treaties with the Arab states. This important tangible political term is missing from both the Peres–Hussein agreement (London, 11 April 1987) and the Shultz document (4 March 1988), which our doves embraced so hastily.

This is clearly settling for less than the required minimum, both in our demand of our enemies to accept the right of the Jewish State to exist, and in our insistence on the area which is vital for our security. This modest approach conforms to the 'strategic' plan, offered two years ago to the Israeli voter by the Labour Party, according to which an electronic fence would defend an Israel within the 'green line'. Facing the rise of violent Islamic fundamentalism, its surge unrelated to the Arab–Israeli conflict, peace 'arrangements' and security 'accommodations' such as these are unacceptable to a reasonable household in Israel.

The Zionist conclusion is, therefore, logical and plausible. It is vital for our security that Israel control the entire area west of the Jordan River, all of 30 kilometres wide. If we defend our country – it will protect our people.

Jerusalem Post, 1 March 1991

Transforming Chaos into Order

THOSE WHO call for a 'new order' in the Middle East treat this troubled region very generously, as if it ever had an 'old order'. The grim truth is that the Middle East is characterized by numerous foci of tension which violently erupt at random. The Arab states are oligarchies or dictatorships, resting on the military and on a suppressed press, and as far as order goes, too many of them were ordained in the Order of State Terrorism. In brief, the situation has actually been a true chaos, which certainly needs to be transformed into order.

Whether it is all biology, solid-state physics, social structure or political systems, transforming chaos into order entails the application of a set of rules with the investment of some energy. Such a set of rules pertaining to the Arab–Israeli dispute does exist, but it has yet to be applied because the Arab states, with the exception of Egypt, have consistently avoided their implementation. These rules are contained in UN Security Council Resolutions 242 and 338, with the Camp David Accords as their special subset.

The gist of Resolution 242 (adopted on 22 November 1967) is found in its Article 1: 'The fulfilment of Charter principles requires the establishment of a just and lasting peace in the Middle East, which should include the application of both the following principles: (i) Withdrawal of Israeli armed forces from territories occupied in the recent conflict; (ii) Termination of all claims or states of belligerency and respect for and acknowledgement of the sovereignty, territorial integrity and political independence of every State in the area, and their right to live in peace within secure and recognized boundaries, free from threats or acts of force.'

The gist of Resolution 338 (adopted on 22 October 1973) is found in its Article 3: '[The Security Council] decides that ... negotiations start between the parties concerned under appropriate auspices, aimed at establishing a just and lasting peace in the Middle East.' Resolution 242, then, offers guidelines for the desired goal, while Resolution 338 prescribes the vehicle which should lead us there.

Hitherto, the Arab states, with the exception of Egypt, have paid only lip service to their 'acceptance of 242 and 338', and this set of rules has been severely distorted, both by addition and by omission. The 'right of self-determination of the Palestinians' does not appear in the text; the phrase 'territories occupied in the recent conflict' is neither preceded by the famous 'the', nor is it followed by 'on all fronts'. International parley is not mentioned; the parties appearing in the text only include states; and no 'organization', or any terrorist syndicate such as the PLO, is mentioned.

Concurrent with such undue additions, a major omission has become habit: few remember that the crux of the couplet of 242 and 338 is *negotiations between parties* aimed at establishing a just and durable peace. The rest of the text, as important as it may be, comprises details, and since some of these significant details are disputed, the differences must be resolved through direct negotiations, without prior conditions at the outset. The necessity to apply this approach can be illustrated by two examples:

- There is an obvious need to reconcile the conflicting 242 'rules' of 'withdrawal of Israeli armed forces' and 'peace within secure and recognized boundaries'. How do you

129

resolve this? Obviously, through 'negotiations between the parties', the 'rule' embedded in Resolution 338.

- Professor Eugene V. Rostow, who in 1967 was US Under-secretary of State for political affairs, wrote in 1988: 'Since Israel has already returned the Sinai, which constitutes over 90 per cent of the territory it occupied in 1967, a settlement between Israel and Jordan could satisfy Resolution 242 if it transferred all or some or none of the West Bank to Jordanian sovereignty.' How, then, do we decide which of the above solutions, all of which are consistent with the 242 guidelines, is to be adopted? Well, again through 'negotiations between the parties'.

We know, of course, that 'geography does not guarantee security', but we also know that a lack of a minimum of geography guarantees defeat. If a government of Israel declares, as some people expect it to, that it would be ready to shrink itself back to the ridiculous pre-1967 lines 'in exchange for peace', shortsightedness will have triumphed and peace will have been defeated. The temptation to eliminate the 16-kilometre-wide Jewish democracy in one quick blow would be irresistible for Middle East dictators, whether violent Arab nationalists or *Jihadist* Islamic fundamentalists.

However, the very insistence on such an Israeli declaration as a pre-condition stands in direct contrast to the call for negotiations between the parties, because by then the outcome of negotiations would have been decided before they even began. Degenerating the necessary free negotiations to a mere discussion of the timetable for Israeli withdrawal does not require diplomacy – a few staff officers would suffice.

But, as far as we can judge, Resolutions 242 and 338 and their Camp David subset mean more than that.

To paraphrase Secretary of State Baker's famous challenge, the following can be addressed to Arab leaders: when you are serious about peace, call us at (02) 242-338. We will be there to respond, to negotiate, and to try to bring, in our part of the troubled Middle East, some order to the violent chaos.

Jerusalem Post, 12 March 1991

Aiming Low

A FEW WEEKS ago, when Secretary of State James Baker visited Jerusalem, I expressed the opinion that speaking of a 'New Order' in the Middle East is a very generous gesture. It implies that this troubled part of the world has enjoyed an Old Order of sorts in the past, but we, citizens of the Middle East, know better.

My claim was later challenged in a *New York Times* article, asserting that 'actually the Middle East did have an old order. It was a fragile, rickety equilibrium, based not on peace and reconciliation between neighbours but on controlled enmity and the balance of power ... If Mr. Bush can simply restore this "old order" and still get all the American troops home, it will be no small achievement.'

The Middle East, I insist, is politically and militarily characterized by multiple foci of tension, distributed randomly in space, with bloody eruptions which are random in time. Designating this state of affairs as 'order' entails a rather free usage of the English language, and a more rigorous treatment would lead to the inevitable choice of the appropriate term: chaos – a violent, dangerous, bloody chaos, with an enormous capacity to store hatred and the habit of directing it towards the Jewish democracy of Israel.

Such a linguistic debate would not usually be significant, unless it carried an intriguing political message. Such longing for the Middle East 'old order' signals a readiness to accept as normal savage behaviour by member states of the UN. If this view reflects the attitudes which prevail in some diplomatic circles in Washington, not too much can be expected for the future of our troubled region. Add to this the new Syrian purchase of Scud-C ballistic missiles, and the possibility of dumping sophisticated American weaponry in the Gulf region, and the prospects become rather gloomy.

Many years ago I came across a story by Arthur Koestler about a dashing young officer who sought the favours of a fashionable lady. To shake him off, she explained that her heart, alas, was no longer free, to which he politely replied replied: 'Madam, I never aimed as high as that!'

Do these circles in Washington aim as low as that? I hope not. For us Israelis, one month after the Gulf war, a pertinent question is still: 'Why, without provocation, was Tel Aviv considered a legitimate target for the Iraqi Scud missiles?' The answer is simple: because for many Arab and non-Arab Muslims, Tel Aviv is an illegitimate Jewish entity, thriving on what they claim to be sacred Arab land. This attitude must change, and towards that change we must all aspire. The American troops should and will return home, but we should not and must not return to the old tradition of havoc. A Middle East alignment which disregards these basics is, for us, a rather dull venture, and a dangerous one.

In my old courses in mineralogy, I learned that transforming disorder to order entails the application of a set of rules. The leaders of the world democracies should insist that our neighbouring Arab states will, at long last, apply the couplet of UN Security Council Resolutions 242 and 338, in which the necessary and sufficient set of rules is embedded. The 338 rule defines the vehicle through which peace should be reached: negotiations between the parties; while the 242 rule describes this future peace environment.

It is important not to be preoccupied with the fact that there exist different interpretations to Resolution 242. Advocating a single, narrow interpretation may leave no room for negotiations, unless the determination of a timetable for Israel's withdrawl to the pre-1967 armistice lines is defined as 'negotiations'. As sponsor of Resolution 242, Lord Caradon of the UK spoke briefly before the Security Council vote on 22 November 1967, and remarked '. . . I would say that the draft resolution is a balanced whole. To add to it or to detract from it would destroy the balance and also destroy the wide measure of agreement we have achieved together. It must be considered as a whole and as it stands.'

As it stands, Resolution 242 talks about 'withdrawal of armed forces from territories occupied in the recent conflict'. As it stands, this phrase is not preceded by 'the', nor is it followed by 'on all fronts'. Moreover, it specifically mentions Israel's *armed forces*, and not its administration or any other aspect of its sovereignty.

In a recent article in the *New York Times*, Professor Eugene V. Rostow, who, as US Undersecretary of State, helped draft Resolution 242, reiterated this longstanding view: '. . . there should be no withdrawal until peace is made; then there can be complete withdrawal, a partial one, or *none*, depending on what the parties decide.'

Yes, indeed, the situation is complex, and it leaves us with only one reasonable option: negotiations. Open, face-to-face, direct, bilateral negotiations, without pre-conditions, with their proclaimed goal being simple: signing peace treaties between Israel and its Arab neighbours.

Jerusalem Post, 9 April 1991

The Territorial Pretence

THE OFFICIAL Arab reaction to the Israeli peace initiative of 14 May 1989 came two weeks later in the final declaration of the Arab League summit in Casablanca. It included the following policy guidelines:

'These are the elements destined to bring about the liberation of the Palestinian and Arab lands, which have been occupied since 1967, from the Israelis, to enable the Palestinian People to realize its long-term national right, including its Right to Return, to self-determination and to the establishment of its independent national state, with its capital Jerusalem, under the leadership of the PLO, its sole legitimate representative; and to concentrate Arab resources in all fields, in order to obtain total strategic parity against the aggressive plans of Israel, and to retain the Arab rights.'

Until today, we have not heard any Arab reservation about this ambitious policy, whose realization amounts to the liquidation of the State of Israel. Up to now, the US has failed in its attempts to convince a second Arab state to start bilateral, direct negotiations with Israel, with the declared goal of signing a peace treaty with the Jewish democracy.

The excuses are numerous and they lead to a single conclusion: the fundamental change in the Arab position, hoped for by so many after the Gulf war, has thus far not occurred. And if the US yields to the Arabs' exercises in intransigence, it is not likely to take place soon.

135

One of the Arab pretexts is the Israeli refusal to accept the demand to proclaim that magic buzz-word 'territory for peace' in the context of the Golan, Judaea, Samaria and Gaza. Some among us here have joined in that demand, under the influence of the extreme left parties and their satellites within the Labour Party. However, anyone who deludes himself into thinking that this buzz-word overlaps the concept of 'territorial compromise' is gravely mistaken.

For the Arab countries, as for other states, the meaning of 'territory for peace' is the relinquishing of the entire Golan, all of Samaria, all of Judaea, all of Gaza and even eastern Jerusalem to Arab sovereignty. From the Arab point of view, Jewish sovereignty 'solely' over the Golan, the Jordan Valley, and Jerusalem is as unacceptable as Jewish sovereignty over Samaria, Gaza and Hebron; and it is ironic that those who warmly recommended that the Taba area be transferred to Egypt have finally buried the concept of 'territorial compromise'.

Going on that precedent, no Arab leader in the forseeable future will be willing or able to accept less than sovereignty over 'each and every grain of sacred Arab soil'.

The gap between the Arab stand and that of the Likud is therefore as wide as the gap between the Arab stand and that of the Labour Party. At any rate, the territorial issue is artificial and it is unjustified to present it as an 'obstacle to peace' between Israel and the Arab states.

Of the 19 Arab countries still in a state of war with us, 16 do not share a border with Israel; and of the remaining three, Lebanon and Jordan do not have a dispute with us over the location of the border. Lebanon and Israel both recognize the international border between them, and King Hussein, in his announcement in the summer of 1988 that he was severing his ties with the 'West Bank', implicitly determined the Jordan River as the western border of his kingdom.

There is no reasonable explanation why Saudi Arabia, for example, is still in a state of war with Israel, nor is there reasonable justification for its American friends to avoid explaining that to the Saudi royal family. The Club of Democracies should demand that members of the Arab League refrain from raising the territorial excuse, and insist that they fulfil their obligation as members of the UN: to pass from a state of war with another member state of the UN, to a state of peace, through direct negotiations between the parties, according to Security Council Resolution 338.

The model proposed by Secretary of State Baker a few weeks ago was basically positive, focusing on the planning of direct, bilateral negotiations between Israel and the Arab states, one-on-one. An opening ceremony, affording photo and speech opportunities, is a marginal yet possible 'addition of props', as long as the protocol does not become the substance. The next morning, the parties will have to sit down to a series of substantive dissussions between them over resolving their outstanding disputes.

Yielding to the demand that Israel should stand alone versus the total 'Arab cause', in the shadow of constant international props, will extinguish the hope for the signing of a second peace treaty between Israel and any additional Arab state. Such continuous props will turn serious negotiations into an international show. In that show, the 'Arab cause' will be defined by the Arab state most extreme in its hatred towards the Jewish state, as evident from the Arab League convention in Casablanca, whose closing statement I have cited above.

The conclusion is simple: the condition for progress towards peace is a patient and resolved insistence on the only reasonable diplomatic vehicle – namely, open, direct, bilateral negotiations, without prior conditions at the outset which are actually excuses to avoid it. Here lies the hope for the beginning of a genuine change in relations between the Arab states and Israel.

Jerusalem Post, 26 April 1991

Alice in the Middle East

THERE WAS a table set out under a tree in front of the house, and the March Hare and the Hatter were having tea at it; a Dormouse was sitting between them, fast asleep, and the other two were using it as a cushion, resting their elbows on it, and talking over its head. 'Very uncomfortable for the Dormouse', thought Alice, 'Only, as it's asleep, I suppose it doesn't mind.'

The table was a large one, but the three were all crowded together at one corner of it. 'No room! No room!' they cried out when they saw Alice coming. 'There's *plenty* of room!' said Alice indignantly, and she sat down in a large arm-chair at one end of the table.

An objective observer would say to the 19 Arab countries who are still, by their initiative, at a state of war with Israel: 'There is plenty of room at the negotiation table', but they cry out: 'No room! No room!', and other countries rest their elbows on Israel, talking over its head. 'Very uncomfortable', Alice in the Middle East would have said, but, unlike the Dormouse, we are not asleep, and we do mind.

Why are the chairs vacant at the Mid-Eastern diplomatic table? The excuses are numerous – the reason is one: the Arab states have not yet changed their basic attitude. They still live in Wonderland, hoping that international pressure on Israel will push it, at the first stage, to a state all of ten miles wide along the 1967 lines, from which the final blow will come. The hope to change that extreme, hostile stand is based on a resolved insistence on principles already accepted in the United Nations Charter: disputes are to be solved through direct negotiations, one-on-one, with their declared goal being the signing of peace treaties.

The destructive diplomatic activity of Syria in recent weeks affords us a realistic view of what an international parley, modelled after Hafez Assad, would be like. Even now, before a peace process has begun, the Syrians are doing their best not only to dictate unacceptable conditions for the framework of the talks, but, ganging up with the PLO, are also trying to prevent others from embarking on negotiations with Israel. Even now, Arab extremists tug at their brothers' robes, and dictate both the tone and the contents. In a permanent international forum, to which one could refer unsettled issues (originating, no doubt, in absurd Arab claims) Arab extremism will play a similar role. Our objection to a permanent international conference is not ideological but rather, practical: We want the diplomatic move to succeed; we desire a successful end to negotiations in peace. But a permanent international conference will become a tribunal in which Israel will be isolated (even if it adopts the stands of the Israeli Labour Party) and in which self-defeating components will bring about either its explosion or heavy pressure on Israel. It cannot bring peace, and the possible scenario was already described by Lewis Carroll 100 years ago:

> 'Let the jury consider the verdict', the King said, for about the twentieth time that day.
> 'No, no!' said the Queen. 'Sentence first – verdict afterwards.'
> 'Stuff and nonsense!' said Alice loudly. 'The idea of having the sentence first!'
> 'Hold your tongue!' said the Queen, turning purple.
> 'I won't!' said Alice.
> 'Off with her head!' the Queen shouted at the top of her voice. Nobody moved.

The importance of open, direct negotiations between Israel and the Arab states is even more prominent against the backdrop of the Gulf War and its ramifications for Israel. We may have become used to others 'resting their elbows' on us, as on the Dormouse at the Mad Tea Party, but it is nevertheless worthwhile asking why, during a war in which Israel was not involved, and which took place more than a thousand kilometres away, Iraqi missiles reached Tel Aviv. Why did Saddam Hussein think that in these circumstances Tel Aviv was a legitimate target for his Scuds? The answer is simple: he knew that for tens of millions of Arabs, and Muslims who are not Arabs, Tel Aviv is a legitimate target because it is an illegitimate Jewish entity thriving on sacred Arab land.

This attitude must fundamentally change in order for something positive to happen in Arab–Israeli relations. Open, direct, bilateral talks do not guarantee this, but they are a necessary ingredient to ensure the success of a diplomatic process.

It is not only in Jerusalem, Moscow and Washington that people should watch their television screens and see an Arab leader (the second, not first one) shaking the hand of a Jewish leader of Israel. It is primarily important for the Arab people to witness this. This is not, therefore, merely a matter of procedure, and in this case the procedure reflects the substance. It is not the end of the road, but it must be the beginning.

The rest are Arab excuses, more or less pathetic, and it is important for the club of democracies not to fall into that trap of pretences. Heads of the democracies should urge Arab leaders to change their habits, and to meet directly and openly with the leaders of Israel.

The Jerusalem Report, 20 June 1991

Supply and Demand in the Middle East Arms Race

MUCH GOODWILL was clearly invested in the latest US initiative on arms control in the Middle East. It was logical to expect that the same principle that guided NATO's quest for European military stability would be applied to our volatile and violent region: the realization that the deployment of nonconventional weapons was the result, and not the cause, of instability. Its cause was the untenable disparity in conventional arms, heavily tilted towards the Eastern bloc. The guidelines for the conclusion of the CFE treaty are simple: a 1:1 ratio between East and West in each weapon category, while inventories are counted through 'bean-counting', irrespective of their quality.

The root-cause of instability in the Middle East – the enormous Arab edge over Israel in conventional arms – must be addressed in any arms control initiative. Massive use of conventional arms was proven to be an efficient method of mass destruction during the Iraq–Iran war (one million dead) and during the recent Gulf war (more than 100,000 dead). When the US proposes to support 'the legitimate need of every state to defend itself', pertinent questions are: how would these 'needs' be determined and who will decide upon their 'legitimacy'?

The characteristic multi-polarity of the Middle East complicates the answers. To show that, let's start with the 'legitimate defence need' of Iran, entailing a certain weapon system in a quantity of, say, W. Now Iraq, in turn, will legitimately need W of these weapons, to defend itself against Shiite aggression. Enter the Saudi family, requiring W to defend itself against Iraq, and the Syrians, also requiring W against the Iraqi Ba'ath. Jordan would now need 2W, but they cannot afford it, so they will have only W and remain vulnerable. Lebanon, a case in point, could have demanded W against the Syrian appetite. It has nothing, and so last month it officially agreed to become a Syrian protectorate. The algebra proved to be particularly harsh for them.

So now, what's the tally, Sam? On Israel's eastern front alone, excluding Iran, the sum total is a 'legitimate' quantity of 4W weapons. If, for tanks, W=2000, the staggering total is 8000, which is about the current figure (though with a different breakdown). Israel cannot afford even half of that. If, for combat aircraft, W is a modest 300, the total becomes 1500, because now we have to add Libya to the game; Israel cannot afford half of that. According to the US Arms Control and Disarmament Agency, for the decade 1979–88, Arab countries in the Middle East received weapons valued at $168 billion, while Israel received weapons valued at $10 billion. Money, obviously, talks before it fires.

These numbers are inherent in the geometry and arithmetics, in the geography and politics, of the Middle East with its Arab system. This system has an enormous capacity to store energy – not heat but hate energy – which has been traditionally directed towards the Jewish democracy. With the supply of first-line weaponry to our Arab enemies, eroding Israel's qualitative edge, Arab stockpiles of conventional arms constitute a major destabilizer. Ironically, it is now to be expected that with a treaty on conventional arms limitation sealed in Europe, major arms suppliers, promoted by their job-seeking governments, will turn aggressively to the Middle East market. The availability of sophisticated weapons plus Arab petrodollars will therefore decide the 'legitimate needs' of our neighbouring Arab dictators, if this issue is not immediately and effectively addressed.

The US initiative touches upon the subject, but must be further developed in this direction. The five major arms suppliers to the Middle East, we are told, will convene to establish guidelines for restraints on destabilizing transfers of conventional arms. These suppliers are also the five permanent members of the UN Security Council, who should be seeking world stability. However, judging realistically from past performance, an expected promiscuous arms-sale behaviour by one or two of them would be enough to put the others in competition, and detach the American vision from Middle East reality.

In the Middle East, where the Jewish democracy is still considered illegitimate, an arms control initiative should overtly tie itself to a peace process between the Arab countries and Israel. In an ambience of hostility, impinging upon Israel's deterrence might lead to disastrous results. An essential element in this important American initiative must therefore be direct negotiations on its implementation, with the negotiations themselves having a stabilizing effect. As peace and security are intimately interwoven, they should be simultaneously pursued.

The Washington Times, 26 June 1991

144

Guarded Optimism in the Middle East

MORE THAN a year ago, guided by the conviction that Israel would rather be criticized than eulogized, Prime Minister Yitzhak Shamir decided to cut the solemn diplomatic nonsense. The diplomatic course offered to Israel was a blind alley in a dark neighbourhood, and we considered it both futile and risky. It is widely accepted now that Israel was correct in insisting that certain fundamentals be preserved.

The United States should be commended for adopting a new diplomacy that excludes the murderous Palestine Liberation Organization from the process, and for insisting that the Arab countries engage in open, free, direct negotiations with Israel on a bilateral basis, without prior conditions set at the beginning of the talks.

Over the last 24 years, three tiers have been laid in the building of peace between the Arab and Jewish nations. First, in 1967, came UN Security Council Resolution 242, which affirmed the principles for an ambience of peace and is open to a variety of interpretations. Then, in 1973, with Resolution 338, the Security Council urged that 'negotiations start between the parties concerned, under appropriate auspices.'

The third tier is of the utmost importance, as it is highly specific and detailed. It was laid in 1978 by Israel, Egypt and the United States at Camp David as the 'Framework for Peace in the Middle East'. The preamble contains the essentials in a nutshell, as follows: 'The parties are determined to reach a just, comprehensive and durable settlement of the Middle

145

East conflict through the conclusion of peace treaties based on Security Council Resolutions 242 and 338 in all their parts . . . between Israel and each of its other neighbours which is prepared to negotiate peace with Israel on this basis.'

So here we are, ready as ever to proceed under these clear and rigorous guidelines. But do we have a partner? At this moment, my answer is 'maybe'. Syrian President Hafez Assad has apparently grasped the international realities and drawn the conclusion that he should seek reconciliation with the only remaining superpower – the United States. He is ready to pay the minimum possible political price for that. The question is, how great is that minimum?

Amazing as it may sound, we do not know. Thus far, the United States has failed to share with the government of Israel the clarifications of its position that it gave to Syria and the actual Syrian response. Assad's foreign minister claimed last month that the United States had confidentially assured Syria that it would pressure Israel to withdraw to the indefensible 1949 armistice lines. Sharing such communications with Israel, or making them public, would have quickly established the truth of this assertion, which now has been denied by the American ambassador to Israel and by Assad.

If negotiations ultimately start, we shall embark on a road paved with cobbles and boulders, crossed by ditches and hurdles. It is inconceivable that we walk that road blindfolded. The attempt to substitute 'constructive ambiguity' with 'constructive darkness' simply won't work, because conflicting 'clarifications' would arise down the road. Therefore, all relevant documents must be transparent to all parties concerned.

We are told that Syria agreed to participate in direct bilateral negotiations with Israel, but we have not been informed of its specific goal. The traditional Syrian position has been that even after they retrieve the whole of the Golan

146

plateau, they would not sign a peace treaty with Israel and would not exchange ambassadors. They would only be good enough to announce a state of nonbelligerency, which falls far short of peace and is scarcely different from an armistice.

When pointedly asked last week, in a *Washington Post* interview, whether Syria would ever be ready to sign a peace treaty with Israel, Assad significantly refused to answer affirmatively, instead mumbling something about UN resolutions. Obviously, from the Syrian point of view, 'nonbelligerency' satisfies resolution 242's call for a 'comprehensive peace', but this interpretation is simply not good enough. 'Constructive clarity' is urgently needed here, and the conclusion of a peace treaty must be defined as the goal of negotiations.

Having developed sensitive ears, we know that the question, 'But what is Israel prepared to do for peace?' is a euphemism for the rhetorical, impatient question, 'But why doesn't Israel agree to relinquish the Golan Heights to Syria?' A similar question is, regrettably, rarely directed towards Syria, which has several times used the Golan as a launching pad for all-out war against the Jewish state. The tiny area – 400 square kilometres – is, of course, vital to Israel's security, but it constitutes only half of one per cent of the total area of Syria. In the light of costly experience, and with the nature of that brutal dictatorial regime unchanged, Israel must retain this minimum security zone.

In exchange for its modest services during the Gulf War, Syria received a $2 billion Saudi cheque, but it chose not to invest it in health, education or agriculture. Instead, it went on a weapons acquisition spree (Scud and M-9 surface-to-surface missiles and 300 tanks), which reminds all of us, once again, with whom we are to do business.

The Syrian claim that it feels threatened by an Israeli presence in the Golan can be treated by confidence-building

147

measures such as early notice of exercises and 'hot lines' between commanders. What Syria should do is simple: decide to live in peace with Israel and refrain from claiming the Golan Heights, which it lost as a result of its recurring belligerency.

Israel has announced its readiness to negotiate directly with Syria, irrespective of progress attained with other parties. Syria would not be the first Arab country to negotiate with Israel, Egypt having signed a peace treaty with Israel in 1979. Still, the Syrians insist on making the Syrian–Israeli dialogue contingent on negotiations with Jordan and representatives of the Arab inhabitants of Judaea, Samaria and Gaza. This adamant position complicates matters, because some Arabs have been demanding that an Arab representative of Jerusalem be included in the talks, to raise the issue of Israeli sovereignty over Jerusalem.

One need not waste words to explain why such a demand is an anathema to Israel. The more they insist, the more we resist. It was agreed at Camp David that Jerusalem would not be included on the agenda. Jerusalem, D.C. – David's Capital, to borrow a line from former Prime Minister Menachem Begin – shall forever remain undivided under Jewish sovereignty. Therefore, to expedite the process, Syria should simply agree to undo the linkage.

So, are we close to a new beginning? President Bush expressed such a hope in Moscow, and Israel's positive response is another step forward. We are definitely closer now than we were a year ago, assuming that all past understandings between Israel and the United States are valid and applicable. The Gulf War has shown how dangerous it is to try and fathom the mind of an Arab dictator through the prism of our Western minds. We live in a bad neighbourhood, one in which you do not apologize for adopting a cautious approach.

Israel has already contributed immensely to the present diplomatic process, demonstrating flexibility on numerous issues. And Israel will readily participate in properly structured talks with its belligerent neighbours.

We are participating in the quest for peace with guarded optimism – we are optimistic, but we must be on guard.

Los Angeles Times, 4 August 1991

No Linkage between Loan Guarantees and Diplomacy

THE ECONOMIC difficulties of Israel arise from an enormously assymetrical arms race in the Middle East. Israel's Arab enemies have acquired massive quantities of weapons from every possible source, and in the decade 1979–88 the Arab countries purchased weaponry for $168 billiion, while Israel purchased weapons for $10 billion. The ratio is easy to calculate but difficult to live with. Recently, in face of the shrinking arms market in Europe, the western democracies, led by the US, have become chief suppliers of first-line weapon systems to the Arab dictatorships, threatening to close the quality-edge which sustained Israel, compensating for the staggering disparity in numbers. Post-Gulf War developments are also alarming: not only is Saddam Hussein very much alive, but a powerful lobby secured a $21 billion US arms sale to Saudi Arabia. The Saud family, exploiting the hike in gasoline prices during the Gulf crisis, handed a generous $2 billion cheque to Syria, and the Syrians, in turn, hastily purchased long-range surface-to-surface missiles and 300 modern Soviet tanks as an opening gesture towards future talks with Israel.

The brunt of all that is fully taken by the Israeli democracy: 34 per cent of our annual budget is devoted to the servicing of debts, which originated in past defence expenditures, and last month, in anticipation of new threats, the Israeli Ministry of Defence prevailed over the Treasury, and its share was increased to 16 per cent of the budget.

With 50 per cent of the budget allocated to guard the house, not too much is left to run it, and therefore Israel has asked the US for aid. It has been a very generous aid indeed, but it should be noted that the Israeli taxpayers carry 90 per cent of their economic burden. It is certainly not easy to make it in our rough neighbourhood.

Enter Gorbachev – exit Soviet Jews. In the last two years, more than 300,000 Jews fled from the disintegrating USSR and found a haven in the single Jewish State. A total of about a million – a quarter of the Israeli population – are expected to arrive, and there simply is not a country on the globe willing to accept them but Israel. We are not choosy – we do not admit only the young, the healthy and the skilled; we embrace all of them, including the elderly and the infirm.

To meet this formidable humanitarian challenge we have turned again to our American friends for some help, which in this case should not cost the American taxpayers. We asked that the US guarantees bank loans to Israel, and with our perfect past performance in debt servicing, this is actually a mere formality.

Last Thursday, an attempt was made by President Bush to create a linkage between this humanitarian request and Middle East diplomacy. Political pundits soon interpreted that move, as an attempt to gain latitude that would enable the White House to 'persuade' Israel to accept positions which are closer to those of the Arabs, in coming negotiations.

This is not only an unpleasant proposition, it is also counter-productive, as it could easily be misconstrued by the Arabs. If Arab leaders entertain the illusion that the US signals a readiness to twist the Israeli arm, they will express ever more extreme and intransigent positions. If an impres-

151

sion prevails that Israel is about to be strong-armed in accepting covetous Arab positions, peace will be the immediate victim. Arab fantasies, that they can persist in their unyielding anti-Israel stands while Israel is to be served to them on an American platter, will turn peace into yet another fantasy. Thus, linking loan guarantees for the absorption of Soviet Jews in Israel to the Middle East political process would be detrimental to the cause of peace.

Unrelated issues should not be artificially joined. Help our people come, and let's work together towards a defensible, viable peace.

Los Angeles Times, 19 September 1991

Back to Camp David

THE DIRECT, bilateral negotiations can be fruitful only if they are free from pressure by the US and Soviet Union and from intimidation by the Palestine Liberation Organization and other terrorist gangs. Perhaps there will be no immediate results, but the very start of the talks is an important achievement.

Prospects may be brighter for the negotiations between Israel and representatives of the Arabs of Samaria, Judaea and Gaza than between Israel and Syria. After 13 years of rejection, these Arabs have agreed to negotiate the implementation of the Camp David framework for peace. Arab autonomy for a five-year transitional period, the heart of that framework, was originally proposed in 1978 by Prime Minister Menachem Begin.

Together with the peace treaty with Egypt in 1979 and the demolition of the Iraqi nuclear plant in 1981, the autonomy concept is a major Israeli contribution to peace.

In the first phase, Israel will try to agree on the arrangements for a five-year period, which would include an Administrative Council, to be elected by the Arab inhabitants of Judaea, Samaria and Gaza. Israel will propose an extensive, detailed series of powers and responsibilities; they will include administration of justice, administration of finance and a strong local police force. These proposals go far beyond mere 'garbage collection', and some Israelis view them as inviting a tangible risk to Israel. However, to ensure positive results at the talks, the Likud government is ready to take serious risks – excluding the establishment of an independent PLO state in the disputed areas.

153

The Syrian–Israeli segment is not very promising. Syria adamantly refuses to define the goal of the negotiations as the signing of a peace treaty, exchange of ambassadors and establishment of full diplomatic relations. In exchange for the Golan Heights, so vital to Israel's security, Syria is ready to declare a 'state of non-belligerency', a sort of cease-fire. This intransigence indicates the Syrians have replaced their slogan of 'territory for peace' with one of 'territory for non-peace'.

Syria refuses at least to negotiate some confidence-building measures such as arms control as part of the multilateral talks. This typically unyielding Syrian approach is aimed solely at retrieving the Golan Heights through the offices of the US. If that is not bad enough, the Arab participants in Madrid have decided to interlock progress in various segments of the talks. Thus, the expected lack of progress in the Syrian–Israeli negotiations might paralyse the other ones. But we should not lose hope. Israel will go to Madrid with an open heart, open mind – and open eyes.

The New York Times, 19 October 1991

Diplomacy of Contradictions

A SUBSTANTIAL contradiction stands at the basis of the United States policy on the issue of Judaea, Samaria and Gaza. The policy rests on two incongruent declarations: On the one hand, the US does not support the establishment of an independent Arab state in these areas, while on the other hand it does not support the continued Israeli administration there. These two negatives do not make a positive, and the combination of the two is detached from the Middle East reality. It is clearly one or the other: either Israel will control Samaria, Judaea and Gaza, or the PLO/Hamas murder syndicate will assume control there overnight and set up an independent terrorist state west of Iraq, south of Syria and east of Libya. Such a development is unbearable for Israel, and undesirable for the US according to the declarations of its leaders.

In an attempt to settle this basic contradiction, American spokesmen sometimes raise the possibility of Hashemite sovereignty west of the Jordan River. Even if such an idea was once politically feasible, it is clearly defunct since the summer of 1988, with King Hussein's announcement that he had severed his ties with the 'western bank' of his kingdom. The declaration expressed a strategic decision, based on the economic difficulties of Jordan and on the rise of fundamentalist Muslims there. Even if Hussein can be enticed by western money to return and rule in Judaea and Samaria he will not remain there for long: a short 'intifada' will send his officials

155

from Ramallah back to Amman. The concept of a 'confederation' between Arab entities on both sides of the Jordan also
contradicts the opposition to an independent Arab state west
of the Jordan. A confederation is established between two
independent entities, and can be taken apart at any time, with
a unilateral announcement from Hebron or Shechem.

The basic contradiction in American policy thus remains
unsettled, and its designers will have to decide if they prefer
the diplomatic discomfort caused by a quiet agreement to
Israeli rule over western Eretz Yisrael, or would rather have
the very real threat to peace in the Middle East which will be
the result of another terrorist Arab state, five miles from the
Knesset building in Jerusalem.

Another contradiction in the US position relates to the
diplomatic process beginning in Madrid. All have agreed that
the negotiations between Israel and its Arab neighbours must
be bilateral and direct. Such a process dictates that the parties
will negotiate among themselves with no external pressure.
The US refused to commit itself to refrain from expressing its
views in the course of the process, yet President Bush announced that the US does not intend to impose a solution on
'the parties', that is, on Israel.

This announcement painfully contradicts President Bush's
request to the Congress to delay the confirmation of loan
guarantees for the absorption of Soviet Jews in Israel. The US
President asked Congress for 'latitude', tying his request to
the peace process. It is difficult to refrain from the trouble-
some conclusion that this is an attempt to exert economic
pressure on Israel during the negotiations. Because the White
House did not ask Congress to allow similar 'latitude' in
relation to Syria, for example, the only moving target in the
US manoeuvring space is the Jewish democracy of Israel. The
additional internal contradiction in this process derives from
the fact that such asymmetric behaviour encourages the

156

Arabs to harden their extremist stand, pushing the negotiations to an irreconcilable dead end, and thus the concept of
'latitude' becomes self-defeating.

An additional contradiction in American diplomacy is
found in US behaviour towards Israel during the talks leading
towards the process in Madrid, and even over the past few
days. Again and again Israel was unsuccessful in anchoring in
writing the understandings reached orally, and American
positions continued to surprise Israel, usually for the worse.
This diplomatic tactic fundamentally contradicts the future
map of the Middle East as drawn by the US: Israel within the
1967 borders, 'with minor modifications', 'rectifications', and
lately 'with cosmetic changes'. Because it is common knowledge that under these conditions Israel will find itself in
morta danger, the US has occasionally offered Israel security
guarantees as a sedative. However, recent American diplomacy certainly erodes US credibility in the eyes of the citizens
of Israel, thus leading to the growing difficulties in persuad-
ing Israel to accept a situation in which its security will rely
exclusively on long-term American guarantees.

Is it possible to continue over a long period of time with
such diplomatic contradictions? A superpower apparently
can, but the result is a series of mixed signals sent to the
Middle East. As we should all know by now, mixed signals
can have far-reaching detrimental effects.

Jerusalem Post, 1 November 1991

The Camp David
Framework Applied

ON 20 OCTOBER 1991, after 13 years of rejection, representatives of the Arab inhabitants of Judaea, Samaria and Gaza, in a joint delegation with Jordanian representatives, came to Madrid with a specified purpose, as agreed with the co-sponsors of the event: to negotiate with Israel on the basis of the phased approach, which was originally outlined in the 'Framework for Peace in the Middle East', signed at Camp David, Maryland in 1978.

Israel will attend the forthcoming bilateral negotiations with far-reaching proposals aimed at solving the century-old bloody conflict between Jews and Arabs west of the Jordan River. The essentials of the Israeli proposition, detailed below, are predicated on the assumption that the basis for the agreement is the Camp David Framework with all of its provisions. However, any attempt to alter the basis of the talks by divorcing them from this Framework will send the parties back to square one, which might prove to be square zero.

At the heart of the concept lies a gradual approach to the solution of the Arab–Israeli dispute. Graduality dictates the deferral of discussion of the more difficult issues, concurrent with an attempt to reach a partial agreement first. It is partial in time, providing for a transitional period of five years; it is also partial in substance, leaving aside, for three years, an attempt to agree on the permanent status of Judaea, Samaria and Gaza. Our position is clear – they belong by right to the

Jewish Nation; we are aware, however, that the Arabs claim it for themselves. The Camp David compromise entailed a far-reaching concession on part of the Likud government: a readiness to negotiate the issue of sovereignty over parts of the Land of Israel.

To be practical, the parties should now concentrate on the arrangements for the five-year transitional period, the guidelines for which are also to be found in the Camp David Framework. Wisely, it was agreed that this period should not be wasted, but used instead to build confidence between Jews and Arabs. For this to happen, an effort must be made to decrease possible sources of friction. The mechanism chosen for this purpose is an Arab Self-Governing Authority (Administrative Council), planned to established through free elections by the Arab inhabitants.

The role of the Authority is to afford self-rule (autonomy) to the Arab inhabitants in Judaea, Samaria and Gaza, and here the precise wording and spirit of the Camp David Framework must be closely followed. With the agreement of the US and Egypt, Israel proposed an autonomy to the Arab inhabitants of Judaea, Samaria and Gaza, not to the regions. Admittedly, this concept is unique, as it derives from a unique situation. The proposed Arab autonomy is thus communal rather than geographical, and Israel must protect its basic interests in these areas, including its natural right to self-defence against Arab military aggression from without and Arab terrorism from within.

In the coming months, the parties will have to reach an agreement on the powers and responsibilities of the self-governing authority. In 1982, Israel put together a detailed and comprehensive list of powers that would be transferred to the Authority, in a wide range of fields of operation. It is significant that the Jordanian government joins hands with the representatives of the Arab population in Judaea, Samaria

159

and Gaza in accordance with the Camp David Framework. Jordan has numerous relevant interests in this Arab population, and therefore its participation in the talks is beneficial to all parties.

The original 1982 proposals will presumably be modified, taking into account recent developments, including the rise in Arab terrorism, aimed at both Jews and Arabs. However, a look into these proposals should give an idea of the reasonable Israeli approach to the issue. Israel proposed to transfer powers to the Arab administrative council in the following domains: Administration of Justice – supervision of the administrative system of the courts in the areas, dealing with matters connected with the prosecution system and with the registration of companies and partnerships; Local Police – operation of a strong local police force, as provided for in the Camp David agreement, and maintenance of prisons for criminal offenders sentenced by the courts in the areas; Finance – budget of the administrative council and allocations among its various divisions, taxation; Transportation and Communications – maintenance and coordination of transport, road traffic, meteorology, local postal and communications services; Agriculture – all branches of agriculture and fisheries, nature reserves and parks; Housing and Public Works – construction, housing for the inhabitants and public works projects; Industry, Commerce and Tourism; Health – supervision of hospital and clinics, operation of sanitary and other services related to public health; Labour and Social Welfare; Education and Culture; Religious Affairs – provision and maintenance of religious facilities for all religious communities among the Arab inhabitants; Municiipal Affairs; Civil Service – appointment and working conditions of the Council's employees.

The envisaged council will have full powers in its spheres of competence to determine its budget, to enter into contractual

160

obligations, to sue and to be sued. It will, moreover, have wide powers to promulgate regulations, as required by a body of this kind. In view of the free movement that will prevail between Judaea, Samaria and the Gaza district and Israel, arrangements will be agreed upon in the negotiations, in a number of domains, for co-operation and co-ordination with Israel.

As may be clearly seen from the above, the administrative council will have full scope to exercise its wide-ranging powers under the terms of the autonomy agreement. These powers embrace all walks of life, and will enable the inhabitants in the areas concerned to enjoy full autonomy. Many Israelis fear that such a wide scope would put Israel at risk, but the Likud government is ready to take serious risks to ensure an improvement in the Arab–Jewish relations. However, it must be understood, that autonomy for the Arab inhabitants of Judaea, Samaria and Gaza, however wide and deep it might be, is not Arab sovereignty in those parts of the Land of Israel, and the time for negotiations on the issue of sovereignty is only in the second phase of the talks.

In addition to the Arabs residing in Judaea, Samaria and Gaza, more than 100,000 Jews live there. The transitional period affords a challenge for the Arab population to prove its willingness to live harmoniously and peacefully with Jews. The right of Jews to establish towns and villages in the disputed areas of Judaea, Samaria and Gaza derives from Article 80 of the UN charter, which provides that 'nothing in the Charter shall be construed ... to alter in any manner the rights whatsoever of any states or any peoples or the terms of existing international instruments ...'. The League of Nations, the predecessor of the UN, mandated Palestine to the British government in 1922, specifying that the Mandator 'shall encourage ... settlement by Jews on the land, including state lands and waste lands'. Whatever final status of Judaea,

161

Samaria and Gaza will be ultimately agreed upon, a 'peace" which excludes permanent Jewish presence in their ancient homeland is an insult to reason and intolerable to Jews. The key to a better future between Jews and Arabs is communal accommodation rather than segregation.

The original concept which led to the Camp David Framework is an enormous contribution by Israel to the cause of peace. It was eulogized for many years, but we now know that rumours of its death have been rather premature, as it is the only diplomatic tool that carries any hope for progress on the road to peace. Let's give it a chance.

LA Times, Global Viewpoint, 5 November 1991

Israel's Contributions to the Cause of Peace

BACK IN THE summer of 1973 I started my PhD programme in geology, 90 miles away from this hotel, a little bit to the east, at the New York State University at Binghampton, in upstate New York. The time evidently was not opportune. I came in the summer of 1973, and in October the same year the Yom-Kippur War erupted back home, which, of course, aborted my first sttempt to become a geologist with a PhD degree.

I came with my family. I bought a car, and one of the things that I had to do immediately was to have it insured. So I went to this nice Jewish boy who was an insurance agent, and I asked him to insure my car. He looked at the titles of the car, and he shook his head and said: 'Oh-oh, Mister Begin, we've got a problem there.' So I asked: 'What's the matter, sir?', and he said: 'It's going to cost you some extra, as your car's plates are from the State of Pennsylvania.' 'What's wrong with plates from Pennsylvania?' I asked. And he answered: 'You should know, sir, that people from Pennsylvania are quite irresponsible; they cross the border to upstate New York, they commit hit-and-runs, and we have a hard time laying our hands on them. So, it's going to cost you extra.' And then came the punch-line, two months before the Yom-Kippur War, when the gentleman said: 'You see, Mr. Begin, we have very severe border problems here ...'

Well, the State of Israel has some border problems too, and as you have been hearing, especially after the Gulf war, they speak of the need to arrive in the Middle East at a so-called 'new order'. This term reflects a very benevolent attitude towards that troubled part of the world, because if someone alludes to the need to resort to a new order, it would mean that an old order of sorts had ever taken place in the Middle East. I have been there for close to 50 years, and I don't remember even one day of order in this part of the world. If I use my background in Geology, I would define the Middle East as follows: it is a part of the globe in which you would find numerous political volcanoes, randomly distributed in space, which violently erupt, randomly in time. According to my textbook, a phenomenon which is random both in space and in time would be rigorously defined as disorder, or chaos.

Therefore, if we must do something in the Middle East, it is to move from chaos to order, and with this in mind it would also be rigorous to say that the rules which are sufficient and necessary to move the Middle East from chaos to order are embedded in the Camp David Accords. They refer both to United Nations Security Council Resolutions 242 and 338, and add much more specific detail to a plan through which order in the Middle East may become a reality.

The Camp David Accords represent an enormous contribution by the State of Israel to the cause of peace in the Middle East. Let us start with the first of the two Camp David Accords, which ultimately led to the signing of the peace treaty between the State of Israel and Egypt in 1979. At that time, Dr Kissinger described that treaty as an event in which 'the State of Israel traded tangibles for intangibles'. I would like to elaborate on the tangibles.

You have recently heard and especially again after the Gulf War, about a new theory according to which territory is no longer significant in this day and age of ballistic missiles. As far as I can gather, this theory is directed solely towards the State of Israel. I would like to test that by recent develop-

164

ments in design and execution of military actions over the globe, and especially in the Middle East.

Let us understand that if indeed territory is insignificant, it follows that armoured personnel carriers, artillery and especially tanks are irrelevant. I would like to cite some examples by which we could test the validity of the theory that territory is insignificant and therefore tanks and APCs are irrelevant.

The first example relates to General Dynamics, which started to design a successor to the excellent American tank known as the Abrahams, the M1A1. It designed the M1A2, the tank of the future, and the question arises whether General Dynamics had been told that tanks would soon become irrelevant, because territory is insignificant.

Last year the US agreed to sell to Saudi Arabia 300 of these future M1A2 tanks. Were the Saudis told that tanks would soon become irrelevant, because territory is insignificant? And when the United States agreed to sell the Saudis some 300 modern Bradley Armoured Personnel Carriers, with Two-2A anti-tank missiles, were the Saudis told that APCs are soon to become irrelevant, because territory is insignificant?

Operation 'Desert Shield' was prolonged to five months, in order to enable that enormous logistic effort to be culminated by the shipping of thousands of tanks to the Kuwait–Iraq theatre. Was General Schwartzkopf told that tanks are irrelevant because territory is insignificant? And when, after 40 days and 40 nights of bombing Iraq with the equivalent of four nuclear bombs as were dropped on Hiroshima, the armoured division of the US and other armies were ordered to invade Iraq and push the Iraqi tanks northwards, did anyone tell General Schwartzkopf that tanks are irrelevant because territory is insignificant?

Just after the war, the Saudis handed the Syrians a

generous cheque for two billion dollars, in exchange for the dubious service rendered by the Syrian 9th armoured division in Kuwait. They did not use that cheque to invest in roads, education, health or social services. They bought Scud-C missiles in North Korea, and they also bought some 500 modern Soviet tanks, T72-M1. Were the Syrian military planners told that these tanks were irrelevant because territory is insignificant? And, when President Assad himself insists that the Golan Heights should be retrieved to Syrian sovereignty, although it comprises less than half of one per cent of the Syrian territory, doesn't he realize that territory is insignificant?

The conclusion is therefore that the theory according to which territory is insignificant is directed solely towards the State of Israel.

I fully concur with President Bush's observation, some months ago, that territory does not guarantee security. We know that, and even the Soviets learned that during the Second World War. Nevertheless, we have to add to this two additional observations: a) international guarantees do not guarantee security, and b) especially for the Jewish democracy in the Middle East, the lack of a minimum territory guarantees defeat!

Having said all that, we can now truly appreciate the Israeli generosity, and the risks that we were taking upon ourselves when, in 1979, we transferred the whole of the Sinai Peninsula, the tangibles, to Egyptian sovereity. We thought at that time that for these tangibles we would receive intangibles, meaning that we would see new hearts, new minds, a new attitude within the Arab Nation at large, starting with the Egyptians. We thought that we could take the risk then, because the Sinai is about 150 miles wide, just enough to give us an opportunity to have an early warning, in order to mobilize our reserves.

After 13 years we appreciate the significance of the fact that the Israeli flag flies in Cairo, and the Egyptian flag is hoisted in Tel-Aviv for everyone to see. However, the intangibles have not yet been fully delivered. The Egyptian-directed press carries articles, cartoons and editorials full of hatred, of anti-Israeli propaganda, anti-Zionist, anti-Jewish expressions. The change of heart is not yet there. We are hopeful, but we have to be very cautious indeed.

The second Israeli contribution to the cause of peace originating at Camp David was the definition and agreement of the Framework for Peace in the Middle East. The basis of the Framework was proposed by Israeli Prime Minister Menachem Begin. The basic idea was the necessity to develop a gradual approach to the long-term dispute between Arabs and Jews. There is just no hope that such a dispute, so deeply rooted both psychologically and historically, would be resolved in one diplomatic move. Both the Egyptians and the Americans accepted that idea.

Gradual approach was translated at Camp David into the necessity to resort to a partial agreement; partial in time – the reference to the five years' transitional period, and partial in substance – the need to agree on what we can agree now, and defer the more difficult, problematic issues to the future, three, four, five years ahead, by which time they may be easier to solve.

Back in 1981 and 1982, during the negotiations on the application of the concept of self-rule, autonomy, to the Arab inhabitants of Judaea, Samaria and Gaza, which also originated in Israel, Israel placed on the table far-reaching proposals. Extensive and intensive powers and responsibilities were to be transferred from the Israeli government to a future elected Arab Administrative Council, to take care of their lives on a day-to-day basis.

Lately, in the weeks before the Madrid talks, we learned

167

that after 13 years of stupid and obstinate rejection, the Arab leadership of the Arab inhabitants of Judaea, Samaria and Gaza have accepted at least the basis of the gradual approach, and are now ready to negotiate it with us.

Our proposals are still on the table: Arab administration of justice; administration of finance; a strong local police; health, education, agriculture, every aspect of life except, of course, foreign affairs and security.

In order for these proposals to be implemented, we have to know that the other party accepts the Camp David Accords, in both letter and spirit. If this is not done, if they are going to play games, we will find ourselves back in square one; and if we consider the uniqueness of the Camp David pressure cooker, I am afraid that square one will become a square zero. At any rate, it has been recently agreed by the governments of Israel and of the United States that the basis for future negotiations would be the Camp David accords, an enormous contribution by the State of Israel to the cause of peace in the Middle East.

There are essentially two ways to positively contribute to the human race. One is simply to do good deeds, charitable deeds, to help, to educate, to be kind. Alas, the world is not yet perfect, and sometimes you positively contribute to mankind by fighting evil, by eliminating evil, and by preventing evil from prevailing.

In this week's Torah chapter we read about Jacob's ladder. It reaches to the sky, but it stands firmly on the ground, and there are the angels climbing up and down. It is a typical and vital duality: you should have high aspirations, but you must keep a firm foothold on the ground. Otherwise, evil may prevail and there will be no one to relay the high aspirations. Even the angels go up the ladder and then climb down to earth; sometimes even angels have to do what angels have to do.

Usually they quote Isaiah: 'They shall beat their swords into ploughshares'. But there was another prophet, Yoel, who said the opposite: 'Beat your ploughshares into swords'! Negating evil, therefore, is doing good.

It is in this sense that I would like to mention two additional contributions by the State of Israel to the cause of peace. The first one is ten years old. At that time, the government of Israel knew quite a lot about the Iraqi plans to get hold of a nuclear ability. We were told at that time: 'Don't worry, folks, it's going to be OK; don't you know that the Iraqis are signatories to the Nuclear non-Proliferation Treaty, known as NPT?' Of course they were signatories, and under the umbrella of NPT, they received a lot of nuclear know-how, free of charge, from the International Agency for Atomic Energy. At that time we said that we had our own interpretation of NPT, that we would do it in the one and only effective way known to us, when dealing with a despot such as Saddam Hussein. We interpreted the acronym NPT to be Nuclear Plant Targeting, and the government of Israel did what it had to do: it gave the order to the Israeli Army, which gave the order to the Israeli Air Force, to ignite and taxi and take-off and fly all the way to Iraq, and bomb and demolish the Iraqi nuclear plant.

Ten years ago not too many people in the world applauded this action, and there is a lesson there, and the lesson is clear: sometimes people don't understand us, sometimes they don't want to understand us, sometimes they are unable to understand us; sometimes we are criticized, sometimes we come under fire, sometimes we have to justify, to explain. But you will find that most Israelis would rather be unjustly, harshly criticized than eloquently eulogized.

It takes time, but ultimately one is vindicated. It took time for the political leadership of the US to understand that our interests then coincided. Sometimes conditions are quite complex, and it takes time for understanding to develop. But now we read that back in 1981 our interests actually coincided, and the proof came last year with Operation Desert Storm. Then Americans were able to imagine what the situation could have been if the madman of Baghdad, while invading Kuwait, had been waving a nuclear toy above his head. How many American lives did the denounced Israeli action save?

So we have to be patient. And this patience, regarding the American understanding of the coinciding interests between Israel and the United States, relates to another Israeli contribution to peace: Jewish settlements in Judaea, Samaria and Gaza.

If we look again at the Torah Portion of the week, it tells us about Jacob after his dream: 'And he woke up and he said: How awesome is this place, it must be the house of the Lord and the gates to heaven, and he named this place Beth-El [the house of the Lord].'

There is a town in Ohio which carries the same Biblical name – Bethel, Ohio. And I think that we should contemplate what would happen if two or perhaps twelve Jewish families were to ask to reside there. Suppose that a certain Mayor were to tell them: 'No, I'm sorry, you can't take residence in our Bethel', and when they ask him why, he repeats what is usually said: 'You know, ladies and gentlemen, we have to take into account some local sensitivities by our neighbours'. Would Americans accept that? Wouldn't the American Civil Liberties Union be at his jugular the next morning? Could any American accept the idea that a Jewish family could be barred from residing in Bethel, Ohio, because of their Jewishness?

There is a Hebron in North Dakota. Can Jews be barred from settling in Hebron, North Dakota? And now imagine, is it conceivable that the only place in the western democracies in which Jews would be forbidden to take residence, to settle, would be the original, biblical Bethel in southern Samaria, or in the original, biblical Hebron in southern Judaea? We do not accept this, you should not accept it, no American in his right or left mind, Jew or non-Jew, should accept it. This is not a Jewish right, it is a basic human right. This applies to our ancient homeland, which others call Palestine, and which we call Eretz Israel, the Land of Israel. It is ours. It belongs to us. But how does that application of a basic human right in the cradle of our history contribute to the cause of peace? It contributes to the cause of peace in two different ways.

After 13 years of rejection, the leaders of the Arab inhabitants of Judaea, Samaria and Gaza at long last accepted the basis of the Camp David Accords. They realized that violence directed against Jews, whether from without – through 39 Scud missiles launched by the Iraqis, or from within – through the Arab violence called Intifada directed at anything Jewish, does not get us out of Judaea, Samaria and Gaza, and Jerusalem. They realized that the enhanced pace of Jewish presence in this area (as quoted lately by the Arab Mayor of Bethlehem, Mr Elias Freij) indicates – in contrast to what their leaders used to tell them – that time is not of necessity on their side any more. It led them to Madrid, on the basis of the terms of reference as written by the United States and the Soviet Union.

It was Mr Baker who said that the United States sees its role as a catalyst in the process, and this is a very positive role indeed. If you realize through Arab statements that an enhanced Jewish presence in Judaea, Samaria and Gaza forms a catalyst to bring them to the table in Madrid under reasonable conditions, the enormous project of establishing Jewish towns and villages in Judaea, Samaria and Gaza is a very positive contribution to the cause of peace.

But there is another aspect to it. In order to explain that I

171

would like to say something about the American policy *vis-à-vis* Judaea, Samaria and Gaza. American policy on this issue is based on two self-contradicting negations, which cannot be reconciled. On one hand they say: 'The US will not support and independent Arab State in the "West Bank" and Gaza'. On the other hand, they add in the same breath, 'The US will not support continuous Israeli occupation there'. I would like to propose that these two concepts cannot live together. I believe that the American administration does understand why they really would not support an independent Arab State in Judaea, Samaria and Gaza. They realize, of course, that an independent Arab State in Judaea, Samaria and Gaza, of necessity and overnight, would become a terrorist Arab State led by one or another faction of the PLO, or by one or another group of the violent fundamentalist Islamic movement named Hamas.

It is an either/or situation, and the United States does not need yet another Arab terrorist state, west of Iraq, south of Syria and east of Libya; we cannot tolerate such a consequence.

For that matter, Jewish towns and villages in Judaea, Samaria and Gaza are indeed obstacles; more than that, they are very effective obstacles; and even more than that, they are the best possible effective obstacles on the road to the establishment of a terrorist Arab State in Judaea, Samaria and Gaza, 20 miles from Tel-Aviv, five miles from Jerusalem. So, as we said, fighting evil is a positive contribution. If we can eliminate that awesome, ominous development of the establishment of such a terrorist state west of the Jordan River, by intensified Jewish presence, by the application of the Jewish right to settle in the Jewish homeland, then this is yet another highly important contribution by the State of Israel to the cause of peace.

It took the world ten years to realize that we contributed to

172

the cause of peace back in 1981, and it might take them another decade to realize that this is another contribution by the State of Israel to the cause of peace.

Israel, as you know, struggles to build a Jewish State 'to be a Light unto the Nations'. It does so in an extremely bad neighbourhood, amidst volatile, violent, hating, one-bullet Arab regimes; it is besieged by a covetous Arab appetite. Its task is very difficult.

We came to Madrid last month with open minds, with open hearts, but also with open eyes. We are not bashful to tell you, our sisters and brothers, citizens of this mighty power of the United States of America, that we do need your help in building the only Jewish State on the globe. For many years to come we shall need courage, patience, wisdom and per-severence, and we shall work for our security and Peace – together.

Bi-annual Conference of the United Synagogues of America, New York, 19 November 1991